RETURN
of the
EAGLE

How America Saved Its National Symbol

Text by Greg Breining ■ *Photos by Frank Oberle and others*

The Lyons Press
Guilford, Connecticut
An imprint of The Globe Pequot Press

To buy books in quantity for corporate use
or incentives, call **(800) 962–0973**
or e-mail **premiums@GlobePequot.com.**

The Lyons Press is an imprint of The Globe Pequot Press.

10 9 8 7 6 5 4 3 2 1

Printed in China

Designed by Falcon® Publishing

ISBN 978-0-7627-4790-0

Library of Congress Cataloging-in-Publication Data is available on file.

FRANK OBERLE

CONTENTS

A s I was growing up, I spent summers at the family cabin in northern Minnesota, just south of Chippewa National Forest. The Chippewa was a refuge to bald eagles during the 1960s, when fewer than 500 nesting pairs survived in the lower forty-eight. Once or twice a year, we were blessed with the sight of a majestic black-and-white bird soaring high above the lake or swooping down to snatch a fish.

What a difference a few decades make. On a recent trip down the upper Mississippi River between Iowa and Wisconsin, I watched as five mature eagles wheeled and jousted just yards above the water, in an attempt to grab a fish floating on the current. At nearly any waking moment, my companions and I could find an eagle or two flying over the river or spiraling on the thermals rising from the bluffs—what had once been a whole year's worth of eagles appeared now in just a glance.

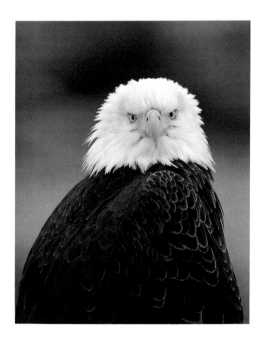

A mature bald eagle—America's greatest wildlife success story. FRANK OBERLE

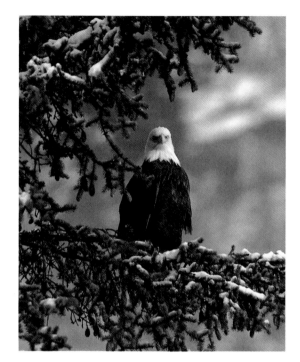

A sentinel of the forest standing watch over the snowy landscape below. FRANK OBERLE

Pages 6-7: *First rays of sunlight shining through rising steam—a dramatic winter backdrop for a soaring bald eagle.*
LON E. LAUBER

8

Bald eagles certainly have come soaring back from their near demise in the contiguous United States. It was the story of their magnificent recovery that photographer Frank Oberle and I sought to tell when we first published *Return of the Eagle* in 1994. We wanted not only to celebrate their stunning comeback, but also to recognize the diligent work of individuals and organizations that had come to the rescue when the eagle was most in peril.

It is a remarkable story. Canadian banker Charles Broley began banding eagles for the Audubon Society nearly 70 years ago, when few people appreciated that the bird was already in trouble. Years later, biologists such as Audubon's Sandy Sprunt documented the bird's plunging numbers. Researchers at the U.S. Geological Survey Patuxent Wildlife Research Center in Laurel, Maryland, determined that the pesticide DDT was the eagle's principal enemy. New York biologist Peter Nye developed the procedure for successfully raising and releasing captive birds. Staff, volunteers, and supporters of various organizations, such as the Raptor Center at the University of Minnesota, have nursed injured eagles back to health. And generous citizens, such as Frank and Judy Oberle, have donated land to provide roosting and nesting areas.

Powerful wings quickly change direction in flight. FRANK OBERLE

But even as we told that story, we couldn't know that the tale would only get better. The eagle has continued to proliferate. As I write in 2007, some 10,000 bald eagle pairs nest in the lower forty-eight (not to mention 20,000 or more in Alaska and tens of thousands in Canada). The eagle's recovery has been deemed complete enough that earlier this year the bird was removed from the federal endangered species list.

Nonetheless, in a world where human activities encroach so heavily on virtually all natural habitats, a species such as the bald eagle is never entirely safe. The eagle will continue to receive protection under the Bald and Golden Eagle Protection Act and the Migratory Bird Treaty Act.

But thanks to the Endangered Species Act, and the many people who stepped up when the eagle's days were darkest, the bald eagle's immediate future is secure. Its recovery is a triumph of science and activism—the ability to correctly diagnose a problem, win public support, and respond effectively. That is exactly what we will have to do again and again if we are to bring other endangered species back from the brink of extinction.

—*Greg Breining*

Playing in the pastel skies of twilight after a summer storm. FRANK OBERLE

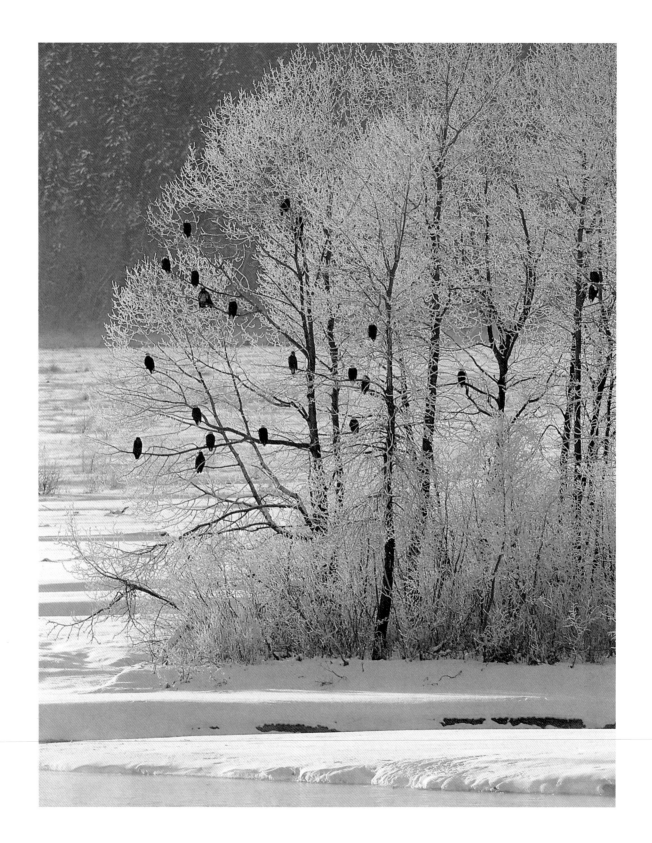

IN A LEAP OF FAITH, John Grobel launched his hang glider from a cliff overlooking the Mississippi near Red Wing, Minnesota. Jaws of bone-colored bluffs spread out below, as if to swallow him whole in the wide gulf of the river. As sun warmed the hills, thermals spiraled into the blue vault of the April sky.

Once aloft, Grobel noticed several large birds soaring in the distance. Turkey vultures, he thought. He enjoyed them. Never aggressive, they often let him fly in their midst. So Grobel tweaked his right rudder, banked his glider, and soared along the ridge, gaining altitude as he sailed toward the birds.

Soon he realized they weren't turkey vultures at all, but bald eagles—thirteen of them. As he approached, two adults—their white heads and tails now unmistakable—broke away from the group. Like interceptor aircraft, they sped toward the intruder. "I've got to get my camera," he thought. But he knew it was too late for that.

One eagle spun and flew twenty to thirty feet above Grobel's hang glider. The other wheeled and pulled in just a few feet from the right wing. Were the eagle a bit closer, Grobel could have reached

Wintering bald eagles perched in frost-covered trees—a common sight along the Chilkat River in Alaska. FRANK OBERLE

out and touched it. More than anything—more perhaps than the fan of the white tail, the seven-foot wingspan, or the powerful hooked beak—Grobel noticed the intense eye, a spot of yellow light as unflinching as the sun itself. Grobel felt the eye pierce him as if it were a needle.

Drawn to the birds, yet not wanting to frighten them, Grobel began simply to talk. He didn't know what else to do. As though they would understand, he explained he wanted to fly with them. He hoped the calm measure of his voice conveyed that he meant no harm.

Before long, the birds veered and headed back toward the group. "What have I got to lose?" Grobel thought, and he turned with them, hanging well back and slightly below the birds to avoid alarming them. The two sentinels led him back to the main flock. Amazingly, Grobel flew into their airspace. Suddenly he was surrounded by eagles, seven white-headed adults and six predominantly brown juveniles.

The birds were engaged in some sort of flight lesson. Several adults would single out a juvenile and escort it below the level of the bluffs, down toward the river, where the youngster apparently did not want to go. As it flapped and tried to climb back above the ridge, an adult would accompany it back downward, sometimes even

14

A mated pair taking advantage of a break in the weather. FRANK OBERLE

A fast and agile opportunist attempting to steal a fish from another eagle.
FRANK OBERLE

bumping it or pouncing on its back. Sometimes an adult would even fly under the young bird, spin upside down, lock talons with the other bird and pull it to a lower altitude. All the while, two adults shadowed Grobel's glider, watching his every move.

Finally, a half-hour after Grobel joined the flock, the eagles began to flap, quickly gaining altitude. They soared off down river toward Lake City, Minnesota. Grobel, quite unflappable, couldn't gain the altitude needed to follow. He watched them sail into the distance, with admiration and even envy for the efficiency and beauty of their flight. For several minutes, he simply glided back and forth along the ridge, marveling at what had happened and basking in the privilege he felt at having been able, however briefly, to fly with the most majestic birds he had ever seen.

Grobel isn't alone in his admiration of the eagle's grace and strength aloft—in Keats's words, its ability "to sleep wing-wide upon the air." Beauty in flight is characteristic of all the world's several dozen species of eagles, including our bald eagle, native to North America and the golden eagle, native to much of North America, Europe, and Asia. For what reason other than its majestic flight did the bald eagle serve as intermediary between the creator and the Ojibwa people? Why else did the Romans choose an eagle as the symbol to lead them to the far corners of their empire? And for what other reason did we choose the bald eagle as our national symbol? Because, simply, the eagle flies with the grace, power, and sheer majesty of few other birds, soaring high to the edge of sight, escaping our confined existence here on earth to become brother to the sun.

Unfortunately, the eagle's mastery aloft hasn't saved it from hard times here on earth. From an estimated tens of thousands of bald eagles in America in colonial days (and tens of thousands more in Canada and Alaska), the population in the lower forty-eight states dwindled to fewer than five hundred nesting pairs in 1963. Yet the magical spell that the eagle aloft casts on humans below proved its salvation, inspiring Americans to band together to save their national symbol from the serious threat of extinction. Through legislative action, research, government management, and the work of nonprofit groups and individual citizens, the bald eagle has been set on the road to recovery. In the process, Americans have demonstrated that endangered species can be saved—if people find the will to do so. And perhaps citizens have demonstrated something more—that in saving an endangered species, they can also find salvation from cynical neglect and narrow-minded pursuit of *more*.

A grizzly bear aggressively defending her cubs from the apparent attack of a bald eagle.
HENRY H. HOLDSWORTH

Eagles at the Chilkat Bald Eagle Preserve in Alaska—part of the single largest gathering of eagles in the world. ART WOLFE

A mature adult searching for rising trout.
JOHN HYDE

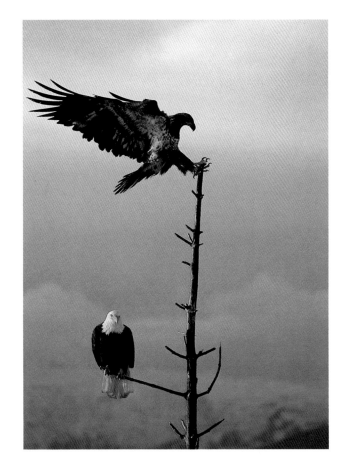

A two-year-old bald eagle attempting a precarious landing on a dead pine tree already occupied by a mature bird.
FRANK OBERLE

The last light of day—a beautiful backdrop for this eagle silhouette. FRANK OBERLE

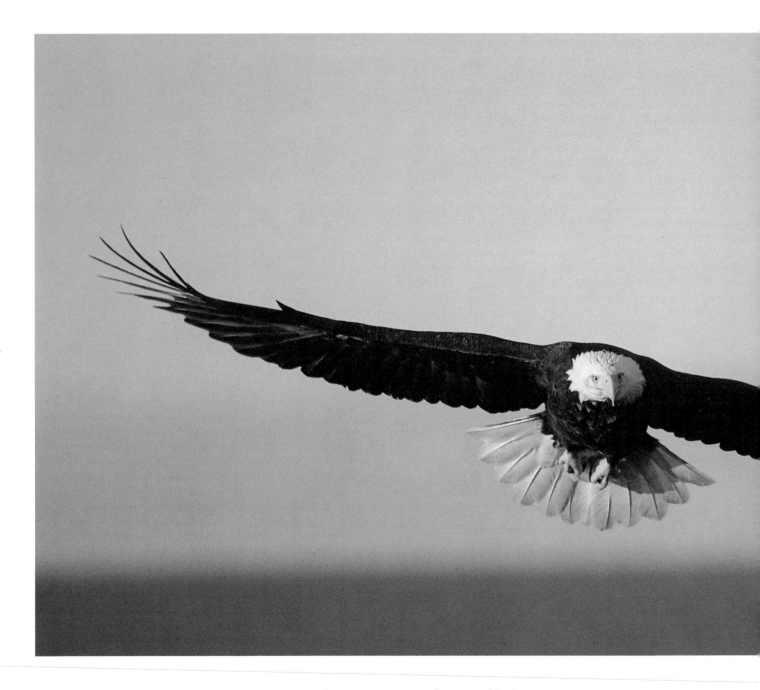

Scanning open water for signs of food.
FRANK OBERLE

As Frank Oberle remarks, "This is America's greatest wildlife success story." Oberle, the chief photographer for this book and the driving force behind it, has spent countless hours in a blind along the icy shores of the Mississippi, drinking hot tea and warming numb fingers with his breath in order to photograph wintering eagles in intimate detail. In an act of sacrifice to the cause of the creature, Frank and his wife, Judy, donated twenty acres north of St. Louis to The Nature Conservancy as a bald eagle sanctuary and viewing area.

"We were a nation about to lose our symbol, and our symbol really reflects our soul," he observes. "If we don't value our symbol, our national emblem, then we are a nation doomed to fail. I think the reason everyone chipped in to save the eagle is that we were about to lose our soul. If we would have lost the eagle, we would have been a society of negligence and apathy and lack of pride. Even though other wildlife was in more danger, it was our soul at stake."

SUCH METAPHYSICS would have made perfect sense to earlier cultures around the world. The Bible speaks of the eagle's swiftness, grace, and strength of flight. Consort of Greek and Roman gods, only an eagle had the strength and speed to snatch Zeus's thunderbolts in its talons.

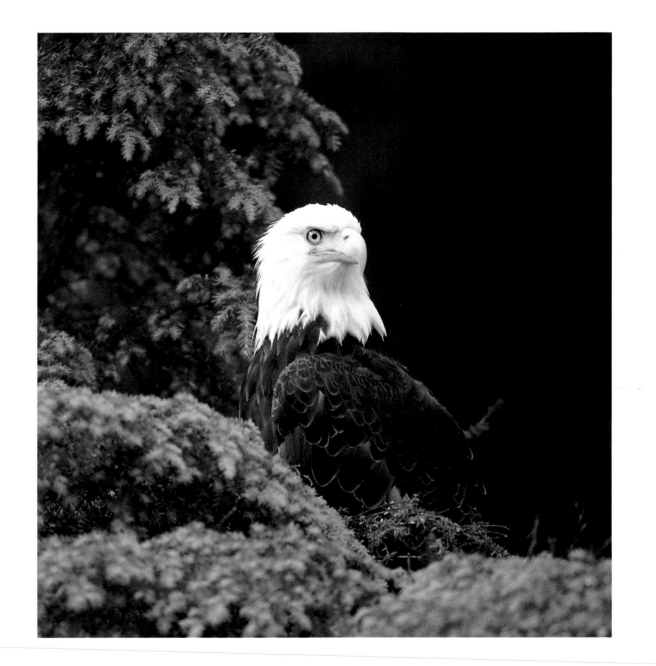

Eagles symbolized power in Babylon, Egypt, and Persia. The eagle was a sign of royalty throughout medieval Europe, from Munich to Constantinople. In Kirghizia, specially trained eagles—a subspecies of the golden eagle—were actually trained to hunt wolves.

The bald eagle, native only to North America, was sacred to many Native Americans. Eagles became totems, representing clans. Their feathers were used for ceremonial objects and headdresses. "Because of the eagle's importance to our people and because the eagle interceded for us at one time, it became the revered, sacred, and honored bird," says Larry Aitken, an Ojibwa historian and president of Leech Lake Tribal College in northern Minnesota. "It was the messenger of unconscious and conscious metaphysical ideas that pass between us. When eagles are soaring above or come to visit you, a lot of people believe they are reincarnations of people who come to watch over us and guide us."

For fifteen years Aitken worked with Jim Jackson, an Ojibwa medicine man. "He did spiritual ceremonies, pipe ceremonies, healing ceremonies," Aitken says. "He was a tremendously feeling and powerful man. I was fortunate to walk with him." Jackson would tell the following traditional legend about the bald eagle and the Ojibwa, known among themselves as Anishinabeg.

A mature bald eagle in the temperate rain forest of the Pacific Northwest. JOHN HYDE

Long ago, Jackson would say, the earth operated in harmony. But then the Anishinabeg did some disrespectful things that angered the creator, who warned that all beings would be destroyed. Hearing this, the bald eagle was alarmed, because he was a friend of the Anishinabeg. The eagle volunteered to meet with the creator, even though the trip would require the eagle to fly very high where it might be burned by the sun.

Nonetheless, the eagle flew high toward the sun until it finally landed in the creator's world. "Who is walking in my world?" the creator asked. "It is Mi-Ge-Zi," the eagle answered. "Rather than destroy the Anishinabeg," the eagle suggested, "perhaps you could send teachers to instruct about their old ways of honor and respect."

The creator listened thoughtfully. "You speak bravely and with great wisdom," the creator said. "For your strong character and heroic act on behalf of Anishinabeg, from this day forth, everything that is yours will be honored and revered as sacred. Your image, your feathers, your claws will be as symbols and messages of connections and communications to my world. From now on, all those who respect and honor you will get special help from me."

"A lot of times when I'm going to go somewhere, I'll get out early in the morning and look and a big bald eagle will fly right over me," says Aitken. "I'll tell my wife, 'Polly, I think Jimmy came by to bid me good travel and watch me.' "

MORE RECENT ARRIVALS to America's shores could also admire the creature. Congress voted the bald eagle the national emblem of the new nation in 1782, five years before the Constitution would be drafted. Thomas Jefferson lauded the eagle as "a free spirit, high soaring and courageous." American ornithologist Alexander Wilson wrote:

> High o'er the watery uproar, silent seen,
> Sailing sedate in majesty serene,
> Now midst the pillared spray sublimely lost,
> And now, emerging, down the rapids tossed,
> Glides the Bald Eagle, gazing, calm and slow.

Yet a contravening and heavily anthropomorphic attitude was also lodged in Western thought. The Dutch Renaissance scholar Erasmus called the eagle "a bird neither beautiful nor musical nor good for food, but murderous, greedy, hateful to all, the curse of all, and with its great powers of doing harm only surpassed by its desire to do it."

Erasmus spoke, of course, about a European species of raptor, not our own noble bald eagle. Yet founding father Benjamin Franklin wrote no more charitably about our native bird: "I wish the bald eagle had not been chosen as the representative of our country. He is a bird of bad moral character; like those among men who live by sharping and robbing, he is generally poor, and often very lousy."

Even when John James Audubon set out to learn about America's birds, science still knew little of the eagle. In fact, on a trip up the Mississippi in 1814, Audubon apparently misidentified a juvenile bald eagle, not realizing that immature birds, though fully grown, don't acquire the distinctive white head and tail until their fourth or fifth year. Proclaiming the bird "a species quite new to me," he dubbed it the Washington sea eagle. A spectacular bird it was, according to Audubon, with a wingspan exceeding ten feet. "The mightiest of the feathered tribe," it was every bit as heroic as its namesake, the country's first president. "If America has reason to be proud of her Washington, so has she to be proud of her great Eagle," wrote Audubon.

Enamored as he was of his fictional bird, Audubon couldn't hide his disdain for the bald eagle: "They exhibit a great degree of cowardice. Suffer me, kind reader, to say how much I grieve that it should have been selected as the Emblem of my Country."

A dramatic panorama in the setting sun.
FRANK OBERLE

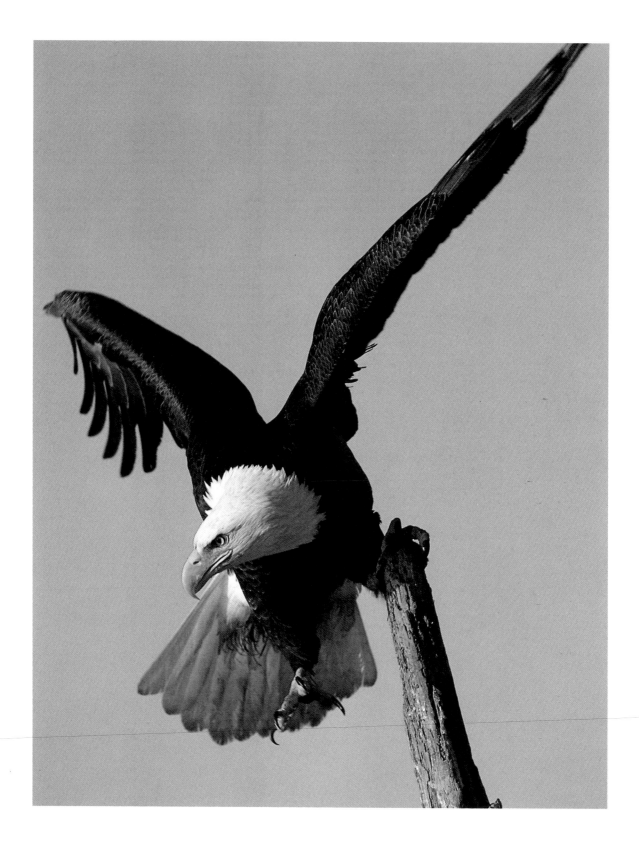

Audubon reported from Florida's St. Johns River on 29 February 1832, "I saw some Fish-hawks defend themselves, and chase away from their nests the Bald Eagle. The former were incubating, and the latter, as well as some Turkey Buzzards, were anxiously trying to rob the nest, wherever they found the Fisher Bird absent from its tenement. The Fish-hawks at last collected from different parts of the river, and I felt great pleasure in seeing these brave birds actually drive away their cowardly enemies."

THE TRAITS FRANKLIN AND AUDUBON so despised are the very qualities that make the bald eagle an impressive and adaptable creature. Not only is it an efficient hunter; but when it has to be, it is also a capable scavenger, thief, bully, and gang member.

Most obvious among the eagle's attributes are its sheer size and power. A large female (female raptors typically outweigh males by a third) can weigh up to about fourteen pounds, making the bald eagle comparable in size to the golden eagle, the only other eagle that inhabits the North American continent, and second in size only to the California condor among the continent's birds of

Taking flight. FRANK OBERLE

prey. (The South American harpy eagle, which reaches twenty pounds, is the world's largest eagle.)

Still, the size and power of the bald eagle are magnified in many people's minds—not just Audubon's. Fourteen pounds, after all, is no more than the weight of a fairly large house cat. And we worry little that stray cats will kill lambs or snatch unattended babies. Yet both are feats attributed to eagles over the years. Evidence suggests lamb killing is rare and baby snatching nearly impossible. Yet the myth that eagles will carry off an unattended infant has persisted into this century—to such an extent that the author of a 1946 booklet on birds of prey published by the Minnesota Department of Natural Resources apparently felt compelled to counter the rumor. "Eagles usually weigh but eight or ten pounds and are known to be capable of lifting little, if any, more than their own weight," he wrote. "Thus only the tiniest of babies could possibly be carried off." As eagle authority Leslie Brown notes in *Eagles of the World*, the belief in predation on human babies "which still persists among civilized educated people is not, oddly enough, common among primitive African or South American tribes."

Though not up to baby snatching, bald eagles are capable hunters. With eyes six to eight times sharper than ours, they can spot a fish from

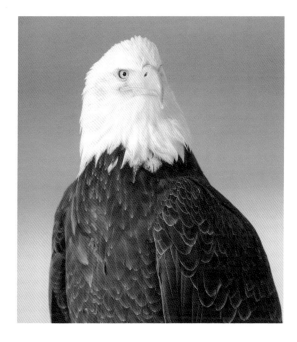

hundreds of feet above the water, or spy a rabbit a mile away, and then dive, if necessary, up to one hundred miles an hour. Even from an easy dive, an eagle strikes prey with a powerful blow. Strong, sharp talons, with nearly the span of the human hand, clutch and carry prey with power. The massive beak tears apart flesh and bones.

The bald eagle's mainstay is fish, dead or alive. Eagles perch above a shoreline, swooping low over the water to snatch a fish floating, floundering, or swimming near the surface. On windy days, eagles may soar above a lee shore, monitoring the surface for fish the waves wash toward land.

The hunter. FRANK OBERLE

A graceful landing atop a pine tree. FRANK OBERLE

Yet the bird's tastes are eclectic. Eagles often scavenge on road-killed deer. On the West Coast they pick away at beached whales. Researchers in Minnesota reported that while most nests they visited were littered with the remains of fish, one contained almost entirely turtle shells. John Mathisen, wildlife biologist for the Chippewa National Forest in northern Minnesota, reports finding a flea market of items in bald eagle nests. Most common are fish. (Sometimes eaglets are pierced by hooks or lures, or are tangled in monofilament fishing line.) Also common are ducks. Mathisen has found the remains of a great blue heron, a bird nearly as large as an adult eagle. But what most surprised Mathisen were a pair of coveralls and men's briefs.

In their world of predation, bald eagles often steal from one another, especially in the winter when they gather around open water and a source of fish. The larger, more dominant—and often the hungrier—birds often will stalk over to an eagle eating nearby and commandeer the meal.

Eagles also steal meals from gulls and ospreys. Typically, an eagle will harass an osprey until the smaller bird drops its catch, which the eagle may intercept in midair or pick up off the ground or water. In *The Bald Eagle: Haunts and Habits of a Wilderness Monarch*, Canadian biologist Gary R.

Bortolotti writes of the following eagle-osprey encounter: "On each pass the osprey visibly flinched, for the eagle's talons barely cleared its back. After three unsuccessful attacks, the eagle turned to brute force. This time coming up fast from behind and below, the eagle flipped onto its back, thrust its talons upward, and ripped the fish right out of the osprey's grasp."

Sometimes the bird itself is the target. One day Michael C. Tritel stepped out of the Carnelian Bay Laundromat on California Route 28. Waiting for his laundry to dry, he scanned the shore of Lake Tahoe, just across the highway, and spotted a bald eagle with his binoculars. Eagles appeared on the lake nearly every winter. As he crossed the road, he began to see rafts of mallards, a few Canada geese foraging on shore, and far out on the lake, several gulls bobbing on the waves. Suddenly the birds near land took wing. Within seconds, Tritel saw the eagle soaring along the shoreline. He locked his binoculars on the bird. For several minutes he admired the eagle as it glided in tight circles, falling toward the lake and rising once again on the gusty wind. Without warning, the gulls scattered, taking flight in all directions. Through his binoculars, Tritel watched a single gull hang in view. The eagle apparently spotted it too, gliding low to the water toward the other bird. The two

Diving at incredible speed toward its prey.
JOHN HYDE

33

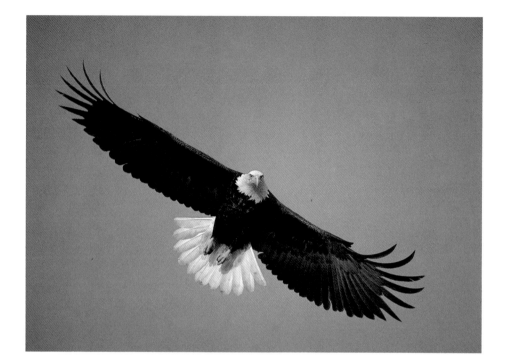

A large female showing her weight of fourteen pounds and wing span of seven feet. FRANK OBERLE

Playing in the warm thermals of a summer afternoon. FRANK OBERLE birds began to circle one another. What a stupid gull, thought Tritel, thinking the gull was trying to pester the eagle. But as the avian minuet continued, Tritel realized the eagle was the pursuer. The eagle swooped upward, half folded its wings and suddenly dove, flexing its talons and knocking the gull to the water. As the eagle circled overhead, the dazed gull recovered and took off from the lake. Once again the eagle dropped from the sky and knocked the gull to the water. Then, instead of plucking the gull from the water, as Tritel expected, the eagle perched on the stunned gull while holding its own wings above the waves. For fifteen seconds or more, the eagle held the gull underwater. Then, finally, the eagle labored upward, carrying the drowned gull in its talons.

Eagles on Alaska's Petrel Island have been known to dig sea birds such as puffins, auklets, and storm petrels from their burrows, ambushing the nocturnal birds at burrow entrances, and chasing them down on foot at night. One observer told of watching an eagle repeatedly swoop after a swimming coot, which dove each time the eagle passed overhead. Finally, the eagle became so provoked it dove underwater after the coot and stayed submerged several seconds—so long, it seemed to have drowned. Finally it burst to the surface with the coot in its talons. Then, water-

soaked and burdened with its prey, the eagle lumbered from the water, its wings touching the surface for several dozens of yards before it gained altitude, and landed on the lowest limb of a tree along shore. Sometimes eagles become so waterlogged they must use their wings to swim to shore.

Like wolves on the wing, eagles occasionally team up. In a valley near Provo, Utah, researcher Clyde Edwards watched wintering bald eagles take turns swooping low over brush to flush rabbits from their cover. Eagles even stalked through the scrub on foot to dislodge rabbits from their hiding spots.

One October day, Jane Whitledge and her husband, Doran, were drinking tea at their campsite in northern Minnesota's Boundary Waters Canoe Area Wilderness when a lone snow goose whistled overhead. On its tail were two bald eagles, stroking the air with strong, measured wing beats. Off they disappeared, over the ridge behind camp. Soon a third eagle flew into sight, glided over the ridge, and suddenly dove after the other birds. Curious to see what had become of the goose, Jane and Doran crashed through the underbrush and, perhaps fifteen minutes after seeing the goose, finally topped the ridge. Nothing. As they walked along the hill, an eagle flapped slowly from a pine. Below the branch where the eagle sat, the

Aerial acrobatics, usually interpreted as courtship, but may instead serve to define territory. FRANK OBERLE

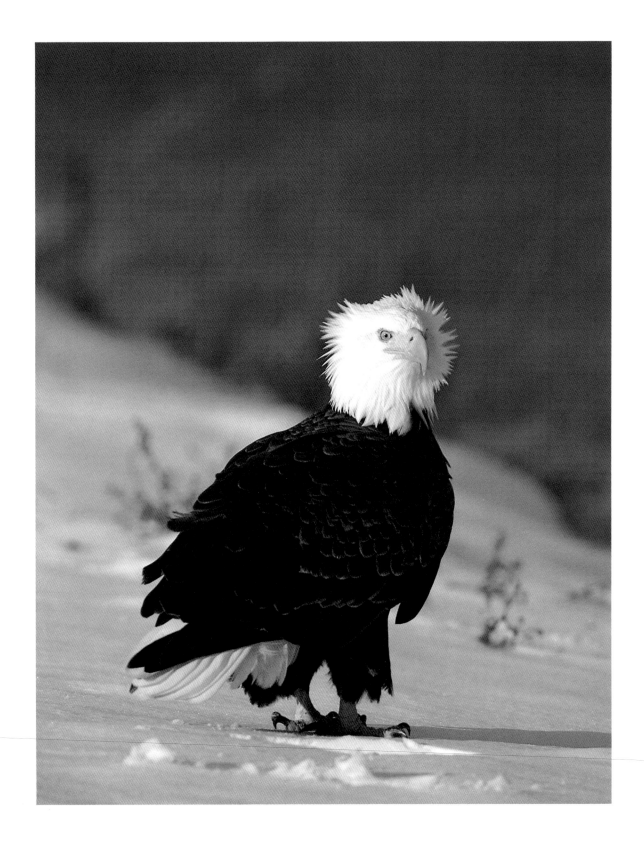

Whitledges found the head and wings of the goose, lying on a pillow of its own feathers.

"They hunt just like a squadron," says photographer Frank Oberle, who remembers watching eagles and snow geese from an airplane over Mark Twain National Wildlife Refuge at the confluence of the Mississippi and Illinois rivers. A raft of geese had lifted off the water, leaving behind an apparently injured bird. Soon an eagle soared into view. As the eagle swooped down on the cripple, the goose dove out of reach. The goose popped to the surface for air and dove again as the eagle made another pass. So it went, the goose always eluding the eagle and catching its breath before the eagle could circle and try again. Soon, however, another eagle joined the attack. Then two more. Before long, seven or eight eagles circled above the goose. Oberle and his pilot flew at a distance, fascinated. "When one forced it down, by the time it got up another one was right there in the pattern to strafe it," Oberle recalls. "Each time we went around in a circle, we could see a few feathers coming out of that goose. By the time we left there was a pile of feathers on the water." Fearing they were disturbing the natural event unfolding below them, Oberle and his pilot decided to move off. But, says Oberle, "I know they killed that goose."

Sharing wintering habitat with bald eagles along the Mississippi River, Oberle has often watched eagles dive for fish and make a meal of unwary gulls. He has watched eagles stoop on other eagles and strike one another with open talons in squabbles over food and feeding locations. Yet the most impressive displays of an eagle's aerial prowess have come on those transitory days that dare whisper the end of winter, with the ice just out of the river and the wind out of the south. Then eagles begin soaring above the bluffs. One executes a barrel roll and soars back up to the heights. Soon two begin to circle. One dives beneath the other, rolls onto its back and clutches talons with the other bird. The eagles cartwheel over and over and over, tumbling down toward the river until Oberle expects them crash into the bluff. "The clinching interlocking claws, a living, fierce, gyrating wheel," wrote Walt Whitman in "The Dalliance of Eagles"—

Four beating wings, two beaks,
a swirling mass tight grappling,
In tumbling turning clustering loops,
straight downward falling,
Till o'er the river pois'd, the twain yet one,
a moment's lull,
A motionless still balance in the air,
then parting, talons loosing,
Upward again on slow-firm pinions slanting,
their separate diverse flight,
She hers, he his, pursuing.

A wintering bald eagle in Tule Lake National Wildlife Refuge, California.
HENRY H. HOLDSWORTH

Eagles' aerobatics are usually interpreted as courtship, though they may also serve to define territory. We don't know. And for whatever reason, eagles will fly back and forth high above the river, playing keep away with a stick the size of a baton. Occasionally one grabs it out of another's talons or drops it from on high and then stoops at great speed, plummeting down, gaining on the stick, and catching it in midair. "They'll do these wonderful little things," Oberle remarks. "It only lasts for a week, a week and a half. Then they're gone. I'm sure they do that all the way back up the river."

WHEN EUROPEAN SETTLERS FIRST sailed to America's shores, eagles soared, nested, and fished along the Atlantic from Labrador to the tip of south Florida, and along the Pacific from Baja California to Alaska. Eagles inhabited every large river and concentration of lakes in the interior of the continent. They nested in forty-five of the lower forty-eight states. As recently as the late nineteenth century, one researcher estimated an eagle nest for every mile of shore along Chesapeake Bay. Wintering birds congregated on the lower Hudson. Eagles were extremely abundant along coastal Maine. According to researchers Jon M. Gerrard and Gary R. Bortolotti, bald eagles may have

Eagles silhouetted against Alaska's setting sun. FRANK OBERLE

numbered a half million before the arrival of the European settlers.

In fact, eagles were so common they were regarded as pests or vermin. In Cumberland County, Maine, according to a 1668 account, an "infinite number" were shot to feed hogs. In the nineteenth century, eagles were shot on Long Island. Alaska offered a bounty on the birds from 1917 to 1952; more than one hundred thousand were shot.

And Audubon himself, patron saint of bird watchers and namesake of one of the country's foremost environmental groups, hunted eagles for specimens, sport, and, apparently, food. He reported in a letter from a trip up Florida's St. Johns River in 1832 that he had "two frolics at Shooting White headed Eagles and killed 5 in 24 hours which is more than most Sportsmen can boast of." Audubon wrote 7 February 1832, "They proved good eating, the flesh resembling veal in taste and tenderness."

Later settlers shot eagles with a vengeance. Barton Evermann of Illinois said in 1888, "Scarcely does an eagle come into our State now and get away alive." Out west, traps and poisoned bait set for wolves and coyotes often killed eagles instead. Not that most ranchers cared, and after the wolf was extirpated, they turned their attention to eagles directly. Western ranchers mounted a

campaign against both bald and, to a greater extent, golden eagles, killing an estimated twenty thousand between 1950 and 1970. In the early twentieth century, Indians hunted eagles—prized for their feathers—to near extinction in the Wichita Mountains in southern Oklahoma, according to J.H. Gaut. In Florida, wrote Oscar Baynard in 1913, "every hog raiser in the county kills every one he can on account of the Eagle's perverted taste for razor back pig." (Though Baynard didn't explain what is so perverted about a taste for ham, he echoed the belief that eagles had a thing for pigs. John Lawson reported in 1709 that one pig carried off by an eagle stirred up "such a noise overhead that strangers had thought there were flying sows and pigs.")

Not only did we shoot eagles; we tried to starve them. The destruction of eastern and Great Lakes riverine fisheries through dam-building, logging, and pollution decimated the eagle's food supply. The loss of bison on the American prairies eliminated a major source of carrion. The extinction of passenger pigeons and the loss of the continent's tremendous waterfowl flocks also reduced the food available to eagles. The logging of Great Lakes pineries destroyed the towering white pines where eagles so often built their nests.

Because of the slaughter and loss of food and

Spotting a fish from hundreds of feet above the water or spying a rabbit a mile away with eyesight six to eight times sharper than ours. FRANK OBERLE

Making a pass over water in search of herring. JOHN HYDE

A mature eagle perched in old-growth forest. ART WOLFE

Pages 46-47: *An immature bald eagle flying over the Bering Sea and Aleutian Islands off the coast of Alaska.* LON E. LAUBER

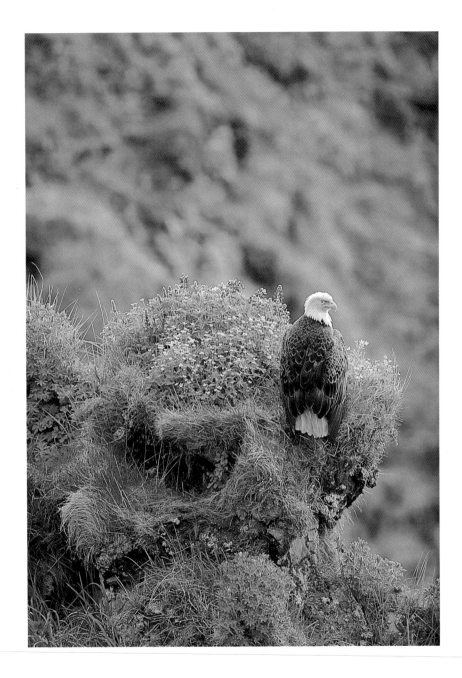

A roost amid spring flowers. Lynn M. Stone

Soaring—with mastery and control. Lon E. Lauber

Attempting a rollover before diving in an aerial courtship display. FRANK OBERLE

habitat, eagles began to disappear during the nineteenth and twentieth centuries. Even in Canada's rugged interior, the eagle was "nothing more than a rare, interesting, and picturesque feature of the landscape," wrote P.A. Taverner in *Birds of Canada* in 1953.

In 1940 the federal Bald Eagle Protection Act helped to protect the bald eagle from direct persecution (except in Alaska, where the bounty remained for twelve more years). Construction of locks and dams on the Mississippi and Missouri rivers during the 1920s and '30s created new winter feeding areas by keeping sections of the rivers below the dams from freezing over. Evidence suggested the bald eagle population of the continental United States was beginning to rebound. But a strange, new danger, discovered shortly after World War II, threatened not simply to once again reduce the numbers of the bald eagle, but to drive it to extinction.

The danger: DDT and similar pesticides. Their deadly effect on bald eagles was documented by Charles Broley, a retired bank manager from Winnipeg, Manitoba. In 1939, Broley enthusiastically undertook a project for the National Audubon Society to band eaglets in Florida nests to study their migration as adults. By the early 1940s, he had found 125 active eagle nests

An easy dive. FRANK OBERLE

along Florida's Gulf Coast. Despite hardships—one rambunctious eagle sunk the talons of one foot into Broley's hand while spanning his face from crown to chin with the other—Broley was banding 150 eagles a season.

But in 1947 he noticed fewer eaglets. That year, 41 percent of occupied nests failed to produce any young at all. The number of failures grew each year, reaching 78 percent in 1950. Year after year, the number of successful nests declined. Looking back through his notes, Broley found that in 1946, along a 100-mile stretch of coast from Tampa to Englewood, he recorded fifty-six nests with 103 young. In 1957 he found only seven nests with eight young. In 1958 Broley drove 100 miles down the coast before finding the single eaglet he banded.

"I am firmly convinced," he reported in *Audubon Magazine*, "that about 80 percent of the Florida bald eagles are sterile." Broley realized that Florida eagles eat primarily fish and that scientists recently had learned that pesticides such as DDT, sprayed enthusiastically after the war, could cause sterility in some animals. Evidence also was mounting that DDT and other pesticides polluted water supplies and eventually entered the food chain, passing from one animal to another. "An eagle is naturally going to catch the most sluggish fish and is it not possible that a cumulative amount of DDT in eagles has caused sterility?" Broley asked. Florida wasn't alone. Eagle watchers in the Midwest reported few young eagles. And when Broley tried to band eagles near his Ontario cottage, he discovered widespread nesting failure. "Our American bald eagle—national emblem of this country—is a very sick bird," he concluded.

Broley died in 1959, just a year after his landmark report in *Audubon*. But "there was quite a lot of interest in Broley's information," recalls Alexander "Sandy" Sprunt IV, then Audubon's director of research. "The fact of the rapid drop in eagle production got people pretty excited about the whole thing. The Fish and Wildlife Service didn't have any money at that time—this was before the Endangered Species Act—but there was so much interest in what was happening to the bald eagle, that the National Audubon Society said, well, we would take a crack at it."

So in 1960 the conservation group launched its Continental Bald Eagle Project, working closely with the Fish and Wildlife Service. "We set out to find out what was happening to bald eagles," Sprunt says. "When we started, no one knew for sure that DDT was the problem. We set out to find how many eagles there were, where they were, how they were reproducing."

Slowing forward momentum to catch a fish on the surface of a river. FRANK OBERLE

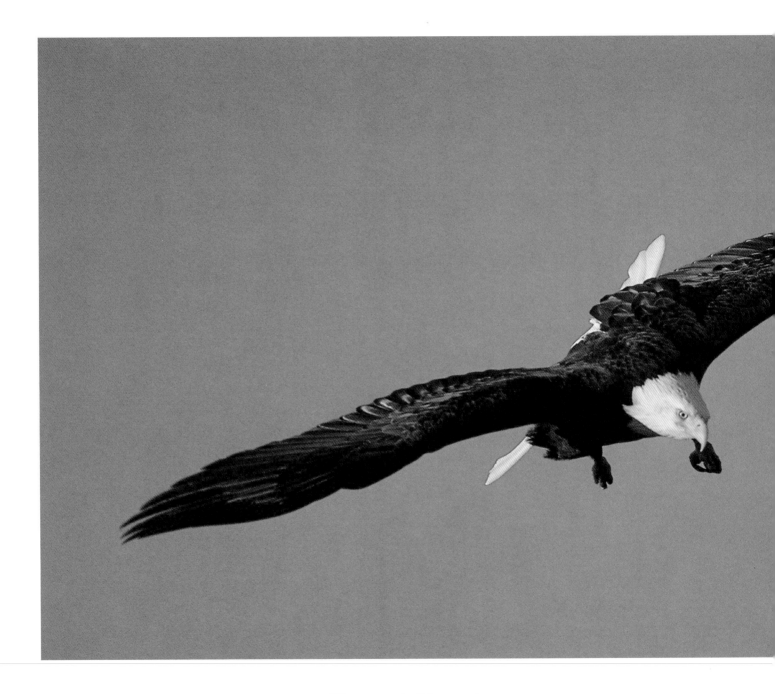

Wings meant to glide. FRANK OBERLE

Sprunt surveyed eagle watchers throughout the country. State and federal game management agencies provided particularly good information about bald eagle numbers and nesting sites. Sprunt also flew over the Mississippi and Missouri rivers to search for wintering eagles and took failed eggs from nests for examination and chemical analysis.

Sprunt's work reinforced Broley's suspicions. "We found out for sure that the different populations of eagles were breeding at different rates," Sprunt says. "If you averaged out the production of a population of eagles and the amount of DDT in the eggs, it was a direct correlation."

Second, the Continental Bald Eagle Project confirmed that eagle numbers were alarmingly low, especially in the eastern United States. In Maine, once an eagle haven, "the situation was very bad. Chesapeake was not too good. The Lake States varied a lot. The birds on the shores of Lake Superior, for instance, were practically producing nothing, whereas the ones farther inland were doing better."

In 1963 Sprunt tabulated fewer than five hundred nesting pairs of bald eagles in the entire lower forty-eight states. The count "undoubtedly was low" but nonetheless suggested the eagle's plight was critical.

The good news, if any was to be found, was this: First, in Alaska and the Pacific Northwest, "eagles were coming out of your ears, like English sparrows,"

55

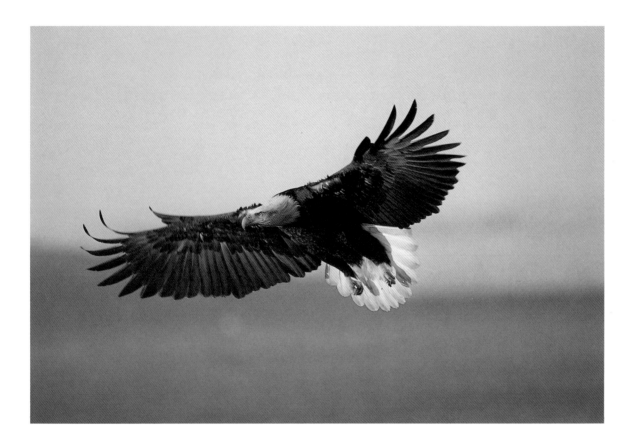

The bald eagle, one of eleven species of fish and sea eagles in the world, native only to North America. FRANK OBERLE

Using its tail as rudder to ready for a swift descent. FRANK OBERLE

Watching over a pair of week-old eaglets.
Lon E. Lauber

An immature bald eagle in the rain forests
of the Northwest. John Hyde

Sprunt says. Second, unlike the peregrine falcon, the bald eagle had not completely disappeared from historical strongholds. However sick populations were, they continued to struggle on.

As the U.S. Fish and Wildlife Service demonstrated through its work at Patuxent Wildlife Research Center in Maryland, DDT and related compounds accumulated in bald eagles. The chemicals interfered with calcium metabolism, causing the birds to lay eggs with paper-thin shells. Parent birds crushed their future young as they nested.

In 1967 the bald eagle was classified as a federal endangered species throughout the lower forty-eight states, except in Minnesota, Wisconsin, Michigan, Oregon, and Washington, where it was listed as threatened, a less critical designation. Because of the designation, federal and state governments took renewed interest in protecting eagle habitat.

Endangered species designation was vitally important to the eagle. But perhaps the most seminal event in eagle conservation had occurred five years earlier. In 1962 Rachel Carson's *Silent Spring* appeared, warning readers in this country and around the world that a "chemical barrage has been hurled against the fabric of life.... Science has armed itself with the most modern and terrible weapons, and that in turning them against the in-

sects it has also turned them against the earth." Beautiful, methodical, solid, and alarming, *Silent Spring* motivated citizens like few other works of environmental literature. Partly in response to the uproar caused by Carson's book, DDT was banned by Canada in 1970 and by the United States two years later.

THE EFFECT OF BANNING DDT was profound and nearly immediate. In eagle strongholds, eagles began to increase dramatically. In the greater Yellowstone ecosystem, for example, the number of breeding pairs rose from about thirty when the ban took hold to more than fifty just ten years later. In northern Minnesota's Chippewa National Forest, nesting success climbed from less than fifty percent in the 1960s to eighty percent by the 1980s.

Yet in many areas, DDT had already caused bald eagles to vanish. Because eagles tend to nest where they first learned to fly and hunt, they are slow to colonize new areas. So, many wildlife managers chose to recolonize former eagle range through reintroductions.

In New York, for example, eagles were killed in the 1800s to protect dwindling stocks of brook and lake trout. White pine forests were logged, depriving eagles of nesting trees. Bald eagles were

Poised for the first flight of the day. FRANK OBERLE

60

probably rare by 1850. By 1976, according to Peter Nye, one pair nested—unsuccessfully—in the entire state.

Rather than wait for eagles to recolonize on their own, Nye, who now heads the Endangered Species Unit of the New York State Division of Fish and Wildlife, decided to hurry nature along. He became a pioneer in the reintroduction technique known as "hacking." Nye and his assistants raised young birds obtained from Alaska and the Great Lakes states, where eagles were still plentiful. Soon they moved the chicks to nesting platforms, or "hacking towers," in the woods. The researchers continued to feed the chicks, which were still confined to the towers. Once the eaglets were old enough to fly, the bars came down. They would learn to fly and forage through instinct. That was the theory.

Nye hacked two eagles in central New York in 1976. Seven years later the two birds nested successfully less than one hundred miles from where they were released. In 1983 Nye hacked twenty-three eaglets in the Adirondacks. Since then, Nye's program has released 198 eagles. They form the nucleus of New York's population, presently about two dozen nesting pairs. Hacking has helped states such as Indiana to restore bald eagles to areas where they had virtually disappeared.

The George Miksch Sutton Avian Research

Watching for prey from a good vantage point. Frank Oberle

63

Center of Bartlesville, Oklahoma, tried a different approach to hacking. Workers there obtained their eaglets by taking eggs—all the eggs—from nests. "In most birds of prey, if you take the eggs of the entire clutch, they'll lay a second clutch," explains Alan Jenkins, the center's assistant director. "If we took a hundred eggs, that would have hardly any impact at all, as opposed to a hundred chicks." A hundred chicks would have devastated the South's precarious eagle population.

But eagle eggs were hard to come by. No eagles at all nested in Oklahoma. So in 1983 Sutton director Steve Sherrod asked Florida wildlife officials for permission to sneak eggs from nests in northern and central Florida, the only southern state where eagles were plentiful enough to risk this novel experiment. Many biologists doubted the eagles would "recycle," or lay a second clutch. And many doubted the Sutton center would be able to successfully hatch and raise eaglets for eventual release.

The task of strapping on climbing spurs and scampering up tall southern pines fell to Wayne Norton, a Gainesville, Florida, tree surgeon. "It's more than exhilaration, sir, it's fear! Often these nests are precariously put into the very top branches, the outermost branches of the tree." The nest, a thatch of sticks that may easily exceed a ton, looks as though a beaver decided to build its lodge in a tree. "There are very few substantial limbs that will support a climber's weight. You test. Then you test with a little weight. Then you add a little more weight. Then you just hold your breath and get on up there." He would wear a mask and gloves to protect the eggs from contamination as he loaded them into a foam-lined plastic pipe. Usually he scored two or three. Rarely he recovered four, and just once he found five. "You don't really have to worry about the eagles," he says. The parents may dive at a climber but rarely make contact. The wind is something else. Once on Lake George, a gust blew Norton from a nest. He dropped the length of his safety rope and dangled far above the ground.

Once lowered to the ground, the eggs are slipped into a portable incubator. After eaglets hatch, they are fed with an eagle hand puppet to ensure they imprint on their own kind, not on human handlers. After two months, the young are mustered out to hacking towers. After two weeks, the birds are allowed to try their developing wings and, finally, to fly free.

According to Jenkins, about eighty percent of the "donor" eagles laid second clutches. And a University of Florida study showed that Sutton's carefully conducted egg harvest has had no effect on Florida's eagle population. Meanwhile, Sutton

Grabbing a fish from the water on an early morning fishing attempt. FRANK OBERLE

66

Poised to strike a fish in the water. JOHN HYDE

has reintroduced eagles throughout the South, raising and releasing 275 eagles from North Carolina to Oklahoma. Hacking was discontinued after releases in 1992 because the center met its goal. Says Jenkins, "We have eagles back in the environment and reproducing."

Pat Redig, director of the Gabbert Raptor Center at the University of Minnesota, has taken yet a different approach to reintroducing eagles to the wild. Rather than raise chicks or incubate eggs, Redig takes in injured birds. Since 1972, when the center opened, Redig and his staff have treated more than seven hundred bald eagles and thousands of other raptors carried in by concerned citizens and wildlife managers. Northwest Airlines has volunteered to transport injured eagles to the center from anywhere in the country.

The center's resident bald eagles, Leuc and Othello, are typical of the victims Redig sees. As I move toward the glass and wire enclosure cage which overlooks the University's agricultural campus, the birds turn their heads smartly. With hackles on end like a punk hairdo, they give me their best yellow-eyed eagle stare. After a moment, they return their gaze to the bright blue beyond.

Leuc was found on the side of the highway near Hayward, Wisconsin, in 1983. He had a broken right wing, apparently after a collision with a vehicle. Othello came from Michigan in 1988 with a fracture of the right humerus as well as an old fracture of the right ulna. Unlike the center's educational mascots, most raptors heal and return to the wild.

Dressed in a white lab coat, Redig leads me through the center. He cracks open a door and we peek into a dark room where several bald eagles, recuperating from gunshots, collisions, and other common injuries, move uneasily on their perch. "The problem with eagles is that they're very wild," Redig says. "They're like coiled springs, and the incidence of self-inflicted injuries can be extremely high." The walls are padded. All the eagles have rubber "bumpers"—foam pads taped to the leading edge of their wings. To clean the room, workers turn off the lights to quiet the birds and wash down the walls and floor in the dark.

In the lab, Redig shuffles through X-rays and shows me the broken wings of an eagle just arrived from Iowa. Shotgun pellets and bone chips show clearly on the film. "Most often we see traumatic injuries — shooting, trapping, being hit by cars, flying into power lines. Those are probably the four major ones," Redig says. "Then we see a lot of oddball things. We have seen birds that have gotten tangled in kite string. We have seen birds tangled in fishing line. We have seen birds that have

Two dominant adult eagles chasing an immature bird from a popular perch. Lynn M. Stone

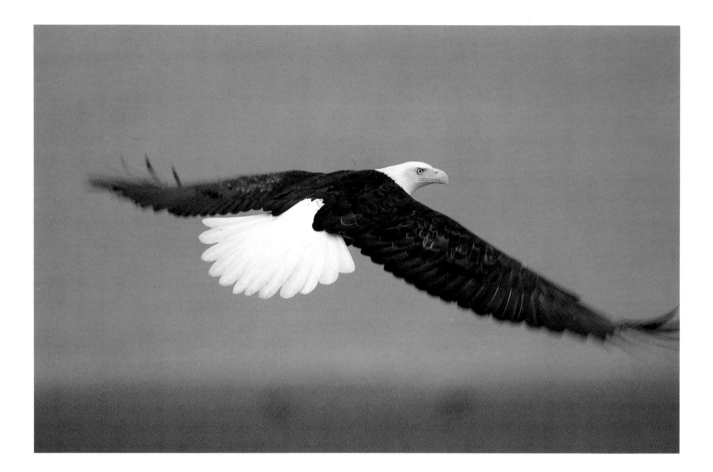

The distinctive white head and tail showing the eagle's sexual maturity—usually reached by its fourth or fifth year. FRANK OBERLE

Soaring above Alaska's Chilkat Bald Eagle Preserve. FRANK OBERLE

ingested fishing lures from dead or dying fish they pick up."

"We have seen a lot of lead poisoning," Redig says. Eagles most often pick up lead by eating waterfowl wounded by hunters. Redig often sees the symptoms of acute lead poisoning: weakness, lethargy, weight loss, green diarrhea. Lead pellets show up clearly in X-rays. This evidence was used by the National Wildlife Federation, which sued the U.S. Fish and Wildlife Service in 1985 to force the agency to phase out the use of lead shot in many waterfowling areas. Now duck hunters must load their guns with nontoxic steel. Waterfowl continue to pick up lead pellets that have sat for years in the mucky bottoms of duck marshes. So the problem of lead poisoning hasn't disappeared.

"Lead is toxic at any level in the body," Redig says. "It does beg the question, is there some relationship between low-level lead poisoning and other injury problems we see in bald eagles? They may perhaps have problems with efficiency in normal foraging so they scavenge on road kills and get clobbered by cars."

Another threat to eagles is the "unholy mix" of pesticides, heavy metals, PCBs, and various organic poisons virtually ubiquitous in the environment, Redig says. One of the most deadly, and problematic for eagles, has been carbofuran, a poison farmers throughout the country spread on corn, rice, and other crops to kill root-killing nematodes and insects. Virginia banned the poison in 1991, after it was discovered to have killed several thousand birds, including a bald eagle and its eaglet. Elsewhere, the chemical is highly restricted. But that didn't save at least seventeen bald eagles poisoned by carbofuran in northwestern Wisconsin in early 1994. A federal official told *U.S. News and World Report* recently that western ranchers use a variety of poisons to kill as many as two thousand to three thousand bald and golden eagles each year.

Other poisons are more insidious. Research on Wisconsin's Lake Superior shoreline indicates eagles nesting near the lake have up to ten times greater concentrations of PCBs and DDE (a byproduct of DDT) in their blood than eagles just a few miles inland. There's evidence too that shoreline birds have a much tougher time reproducing. Other research suggests that many pesticides and complex industrial pollutants mimic the effects of estrogens and other natural hormones that control bodily development. Their presence may cause birth defects, infertility, and other abnormalities—not only in bald eagles and other wildlife, but also, perhaps, in humans.

Serious though these problems are, they've not prevented a bald eagle recovery, Redig observes.

Parachuting to grab a fish from the water.
FRANK OBERLE

Gliding effortlessly through the sky.
FRANK OBERLE

"The bald eagle population, despite all that, with the management protection given to it under the Endangered Species Act, has done incredibly well."

Periodically, the Raptor Center releases its recovered raptors. Besides making terrific photo opportunities, the sight of an eagle flying free once more provides infinite rewards to the 150 volunteers who donate twenty thousand hours to the center each year, swabbing out bird quarters and leading tours. "This is an avenue of involvement for them with conservation," Redig says. "They become real advocates for what we're doing. I make no arguments at all that the rehabilitation work we've done has had any direct impact on the bald eagle population. But it has had a tremendous impact on people's attitudes, understanding, and appreciation for bald eagles and the very nature of the problems we do unwittingly create."

W HEN CHARLES BROLEY first banded eagles in Florida, he noted the explosion of housing developments in prime eagle nesting areas. He dismissed the loss of habitat as "a minor factor" in comparison to DDT poisoning. But as the threat of DDT has diminished and humans' appetite for land increases, the ravening plunder of the eagles' habitat has become the most serious threat.

Since Broley's pioneering work, eagle nesting and nesting habitat have most concerned conservationists. Important early work occurred in the Chippewa National Forest, along the headwaters of the Mississippi, where the river is a rippling forest stream with little evidence of its impending grandeur. This tall-pine and lake country has one of the highest densities of breeding eagles in the United States. Even during the dark days of the 1950s and '60s, the 1.6-million-acre Chippewa harbored more than twenty pairs of breeding birds.

Eagles shared the Chippewa with loggers, fishermen, cabin owners, and tourists. John Mathisen, the forest's young biologist, knew it was vital to protect this eagle nesting stronghold from disturbance. He realized that loss of nesting trees could seriously affect the eagle population. The construction of logging roads and even disturbance by hikers and campers could drive eagles away from a nest.

So in the early 1960s, Mathisen began to track the number and nesting success of bald eagles in the forest. He also began to develop a method of protecting individual bald eagle nests that serves as a model for many land management agencies today.

Mathisen recorded the precise location of each nest. Most sat in the so-called supercanopy white pine and red pine—the aged giants that tower above the other trees of the forest. Often the uppermost branches were dead and bare, providing a platform for the huge nest and landing space for an incoming bird with a seven-foot wingspan. Usually the eagles chose a tree near a lake or open meadow. For each nest, Mathisen noted the type and size of tree that supported it, described the surrounding habitat, and identified nearby activities, such as logging or recreation, that might disturb nesting eagles. He'd even take low-level aerial photos to establish a record of the forest cover and land use. Finally, he'd establish a buffer zone around each nest, permitting no activity at all within one hundred meters, and some restrictions, especially during nesting, up to a half-mile away. Though laborious and time-consuming, the protection has paid off, says Mathisen. Once DDT was banned, the number of nesting eagles increased nearly tenfold, to almost two hundred pairs by 1993.

Federal and state agencies have acted to protect nesting eagles on public land. Yet many prime nesting spots occupy private ground, where they may be lost to logging or development. Often, government hasn't been able to act quickly enough to spare the land. Sometimes, agencies are simply too broke to buy. Fortunately, private conservation

Five adult birds taking advantage of a raised perch. LYNN M. STONE

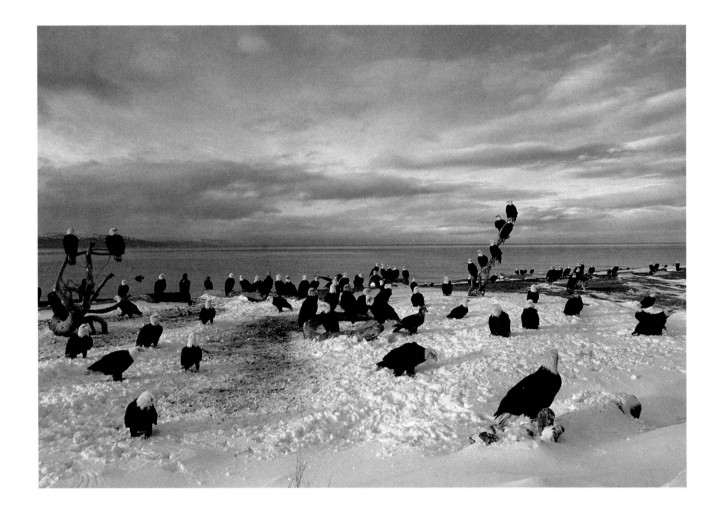

groups such as The Nature Conservancy have often stepped forward to buy land to protect it.

Along Maine's craggy seacoast, where flocks of bald eagles once soared, pesticides nearly destroyed the population. In 1965 four eaglets fledged in Maine. Recovery has been slow. Barely more than one hundred eagles survive today. The Nature Conservancy has been working with the Maine Coast Heritage Trust, local towns, private landowners, and the Maine Bureau of Public Lands and Department of Inland Fisheries and Wildlife to protect the forty-five islands of the Great Wass Island Archipelago. The Conservancy itself has purchased and protected more than a dozen islands with bald eagle nesting and summer roosting sites.

The Conservancy's Louisiana Field Office recently purchased 547 acres just outside New Orleans to establish its White Kitchen Preserve, a sprawling complex of freshwater marsh and cypress-tupelo swamp named for the restaurant that once overlooked the property from U.S. 90. High up in one tree is a stick nest the size of a Volkswagen, tended for seventy years by successive generations of bald eagles.

The Conservancy's Virginia Chapter raised nearly $2 million to buy 3,500 acres along the James River near Hopewell. The land has been sold to the U.S. Fish and Wildlife Service and, with recent additions of land, now forms the James River National Wildlife Refuge. Surrounded by burgeoning development spreading out from Richmond, the refuge harbors three active bald eagle nests and more than 125 roosting and feeding eagles during the summer, making it one of the largest summer roosts in the eastern United States.

In Michigan's Upper Peninsula, Ford Motor Company will continue to lease sixty-seven acres to the Conservancy for as long as eagles nest on the site. The Conservancy's Michigan chapter also protects 2,168 acres of bald eagle habitat in its Erie Marsh Preserve. But emblematic of the Great Lakes' continuing pollution problems, the first eaglet produced on the site in years was born with a crossed-over bill. The deformity, probably caused by contaminants in fish, would have doomed the eaglet to starve had it been left in the wild.

The Conservancy protects bald eagle habitat in other states as well. The organization purchased 1,889-acre Otter Island for the South Carolina Wildlife and Marine Resources Department. The Oklahoma Chapter has teamed up with local Audubon chapters and state and federal agencies to establish the Arkansas River Bald Eagle Preserve. Landowners sign a nonbinding registry agreement indicating they won't alter eagle habitat. A recent registry now

Part of the November-December congregation of 5,000 bald eagles along the Chilkat River, Alaska. LYNN M. STONE

supports a nest built by two eagles raised and released several years ago by the George Miksch Sutton Avian Research Center.

Florida, location of some of the country's most intense development pressure, is home also to some of its most extensive eagle nesting preserves. Working with local watershed management districts, the state, and the U.S. Fish and Wildlife Service, the Conservancy has helped protect hundreds of thousands of acres of lake and river shoreline, marshes, and swamps that provide habitat for bald eagles, Florida panthers, and other endangered creatures.

The organization worked with the Walt Disney World Co. to protect 8,500 acres of pine flatwoods, oak scrub, and mesic hammocks lying between Lake Russell and Lake Hatchineha south of Orlando. With new additions of land, the site, now called Disney Wilderness Preserve, will total more than eleven thousand acres. Six pairs of bald eagles nest on the property. The site also provides habitat for the federally endangered wood stork, and the federally threatened Florida scrub jay, crested caracara, eastern indigo snake, and American alligator.

The preserve got its start when Disney asked state, federal, and local authorities permission to develop 500 acres of wetlands at Walt Disney

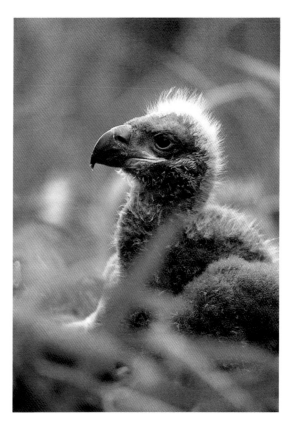

A 23-day-old eaglet waiting for a parent to bring its next meal to the nest. Lon E. Lauber

A fledgling bald eagle and its mother in a nest at Cross Lake, Minnesota. Eugene F. O'Neill

81

World. Agencies approved—if Disney agreed to purchase what was then known as Walker Ranch, a working cattle ranch and hunting camp being held for commercial development. Disney bought the land in 1992 and is turning ownership over to the Conservancy in stages. The conservation group plans to build an environmental learning center on the site.

The Disney preserve is flanked by residential and commercial development. From his office window, preserve director Steve Gatewood watches homes go up. The surrounding population will complicate the Conservancy's efforts to manage meadows and scrub lands with controlled burning. On the bright side, says Gatewood, "We're going to have a neighborhood constituency. We're going to recruit some of those people to volunteer here and become the advocates to protect the preserve."

NO LESS IMPORTANT TO EAGLES than their nesting sites are the areas where they gather in winter by the dozens or hundreds to catch fish during the day and roost by night in trees protected from icy northern blasts. Each autumn in Montana, for example, resource management agencies prohibit boating, walking, or driving within three miles downstream of the Canyon

An eagle in flight—the embodiment of elegance, strength, and nobility. FRANK OBERLE

Ferry Dam near Helena, where up to three hundred bald eagles gather to feed on spawned-out and dying kokanee salmon.

Another such oasis occurs at Keokuk, Iowa, where the mighty Mississippi churns through the hydro plant at Lock and Dam No. 19, masticating gizzard shad and remaining blessedly ice-free all winter. Eagles from Canada, Minnesota, and Wisconsin flock southward and park at Keokuk for the winter, sometimes four hundred strong, to dine on floating, headless shad and sleep in the welcoming trees of a nearby coulee on the Illinois shore.

The coulee is called Cedar Glen Eagle Roost. In 1979, The Nature Conservancy purchased nearly nine hundred acres to provide safe haven for wintering eagles—perhaps the first winter sanctuary established in the country. Since then several hundred additional acres have been purchased to protect the old hardwood roost trees from logging and provide protection from intrusive humans, including the thousands of eagle watchers that now flock to the area every winter. Humans must stay off the preserve from November through February when eagles are most numerous. After the birds go north, the Friends of Cedar Creek volunteer their time to tend to the trails and care for native vegetation.

The Conservancy and other organizations have worked with public agencies to protect other important roosting sites across the country:

One such area lies along the South Fork of the Snake River, where the stream spills from the deep folds of the Tetons into a wide valley of cottonwoods, Douglas fir, aspens, and wetlands. With abundant trout and thousands of wintering waterfowl, the sheltered canyon harbors the greatest concentration of nesting and wintering eagles in the greater Yellowstone region. Some residents saw a chance to cash in on the demand for homesites in this popular tourist area. One South Fork landowner even obtained the permits necessary to built sixty-six homes, a golf course, and a jet-boat marina. Outraged residents tried but failed to stop the development, so the Conservancy stepped in to buy land along twenty-five miles of the river to keep it wild. Federal agencies, groups such as the National Fish and Wildlife Foundation, and sympathetic individual buyers have joined in. Now about 90 percent of the river corridor is protected from further development.

In Wyoming, ranchers Oliver and Deborah Scott gave the Conservancy a conservation easement to protect seven thousand acres of prairie and woodland flanking the North Platte River where eagles roost and fish each winter.

Using great strength and mighty wings to reach the cold winter sky for the first hunt of the day. FRANK OBERLE

The Conservancy's Montana field office is working with the Confederated Salish and Kootenai Tribes of the Flathead Reservation to protect and manage a marshy bald eagle roost on the shores of Flathead Lake.

The National Wildlife Federation donated 150 acres along the Wisconsin River to protect wintering habitat in Wisconsin.

Along Washington's Skagit River, where several hundred eagles gather in winter to feed on spawned-out salmon, The Nature Conservancy negotiated with private landowners to increase the size of a state-owned preserve along the river. A proposal by the city of Seattle to build a hydroelectric project on the Skagit was quickly shelved after a study showed a dam and impoundment would diminish the salmon run and the eagles' winter food supply. Indeed, the Seattle utility has provided money to buy additional land and extend the preserve along the Skagit.

Farther south hundreds of wintering bald eagles congregate in the Klamath Basin, straddling the Oregon-California border. The Conservancy bought more than one thousand acres, which it sold to the U.S. Fish and Wildlife Service to include in the Bear Valley National Wildlife Refuge.

Nowhere else do bald eagles gather as they do along the coasts of British Columbia and southeastern Alaska. The granddaddy of all wintering refuges is the 48,000-acre Chilkat Bald Eagle Preserve near Haines, Alaska, where the state's panhandle meets the pan. As the Chilkat River approaches the Pacific, it spreads out in a broad flat. Ground-temperature water stored in the alluvial gravel seeps into the Chilkat, keeping it open all year. Up to three thousand eagles gather along the river, like rapacious fishermen wading into the shallows to snatch dying chum salmon drifting in the current. The state established the preserve in 1982 to protect the largest gathering of wintering bald eagles in existence. A small donation of land, made through The Nature Conservancy, added to extensive state holdings.

EVERY FALL THOUSANDS OF RAPTORS and other birds spill from the boreal forest of Canada and northern Minnesota and funnel along the northern shore of Lake Superior, aided in their migration by strong winds pushing them southward and by the thermals and updrafts lifting them above the rocky shore. Since the early 1950s, volunteers of the Duluth Audubon Society have gathered on Hawk Ridge, which rises above Superior's sparkling shore on the outskirts of town, to carefully count and tabulate the number of eagles and other large birds.

A mated pair of bald eagles. FRANK OBERLE

A nesting bald eagle at the Disney Wilderness Preserve in Florida. Lynda Richardson

A mature adult with a freshly caught kokanee salmon from the Missouri River in Montana. Steve Justad

During the '50s and '60s, the numbers of many raptors, including bald eagles, remained sparse. In 1953 and 1959, spotters saw no bald eagles at all. But beginning in about 1980, the numbers rose dramatically. In 1993, volunteers sighted 1,725, double the previous record.

No doubt about it, the bald eagle is back. During the past twenty years, its numbers have increased in every part of the continent. From Sandy Sprunt's count of fewer than 500 nesting pairs in 1963, the number of nesting pairs in the lower forty-eight states has increased to more than four thousand, according to the U.S. Fish and Wildlife Service. Counting juvenile birds, the number of bald eagles may total sixteen thousand. Alaskan and Canadian populations add several tens of thousands more.

The bald eagle is becoming so plentiful and widespread, it is even returning to nesting and roosting sites crowded by homes and offices.

"There has been a lot of education going on, with people learning to cohabit with these birds," says Joan Galli, ecologist with the nongame program for the Minnesota Department of Natural Resources. "You might be surprised that they would be so close to people."

Galli and I drive among the complex of lakes, marshes, and scattered woods just a few miles north of Minneapolis and St. Paul. Two decades ago, eagles were rarely seen in this part of the state. This year, about 20 pairs nest in the metropolitan area. "If you look at where they're nesting, it seems to me that for the most part they are still in islands of habitat that have a remoteness to them," Galli says. "From an eagle-eye perspective, those spots are pretty easy to find."

Galli stops the van, pulling fully onto the shoulder to avoid the steady traffic. She sets up a spotting scope on the gravel, turns it to a spreading white pine on the shore of a small lake, and stands aside so I can look. An adult eagle fidgets in a nest, shifting its weight from foot to foot. Suddenly the head of an eaglet pops up among the branches. "Eagles have learned a little adaptability, and people have learned to be tolerant of them and more courteous of them and more considerate," Galli says. In one instance, eagles have nested in a white pine growing in a suburban homeowner's backyard. Others nest in the flight path of planes using Minneapolis-St. Paul International Airport.

I recalled one spring when I walked along the Mississippi in the Katharine Ordway Natural History Study Area with David Clugston, who was then the resident naturalist. The private reserve borders River Lake, a backwater just downstream from the Twin Cities. "Just this year I found a

An eagle preparing to land and wait out a storm. FRANK OBERLE

91

beaver lodge on the end of that peninsula and also some giant floater clams, which aren't supposed to be here because of the water quality," Clugston said. "Those are hopeful signs that the water quality is improving, but we have a long way to go." As he finished, I looked up to see a bald eagle soar into the branches of a tree by the river. Moments later, it was joined by another. All this fewer than ten miles from St. Paul.

For several years, that encounter stood as my quintessential urban eagle experience. But just the other day I glanced out my office window and noticed a bald eagle lazily flapping over downtown St. Paul, heading north with the other afternoon commuters on Interstate 35E.

BECAUSE THE EAGLE has fared so well, the U.S. Fish and Wildlife Service upgraded the bird's status in 1994 from endangered to threatened throughout the lower forty-eight states. The prognosis? "Right now it looks terrific," says Jody Millar, national recovery coordinator for the Fish and Wildlife Service in Rock Island, Illinois. "The eagle has made remarkable recovery since it was first protected."

The bald eagle is one of relatively few creatures on the endangered species list to show

Beginning a power dive to assert dominance over another eagle. FRANK OBERLE

improvement, much less hope of recovery. Others include the gray wolf and American alligator. More typical, however, are the California condor and Florida panther, which number so few their future is in grave doubt.

Why has the eagle fared relatively well, when other species have continued to slip deeper into the chasm of extinction?

First, the threat of DDT, though serious, was singular and relatively easy to eliminate. "To find one major causal agent is a blessing," says Millar. Far tougher than banning a single family of pesticides is attacking the multifarious problems of habitat destruction, competition from exotic species, and chronic poisoning by industrial contaminants—the combination that plagues many other species.

Second, bald eagles enjoyed a wide distribution and could adapt to a range of foods and habitats. Eliminating the birds from one area— such as much of the industrial East, Midwest, and South—didn't doom them. Eagles continued to thrive elsewhere on the continent.

Finally, it's easier to love a bald eagle than a dwarf wedge mussel or a Jessup's milk vetch. As fund-raisers of conservation groups know only too well, eagles, wolves, and whales speak to people. Conservationists even have a name for these glamour species: charismatic megafauna. And the eagle is nothing if not charismatic and mega.

What has the recovery of the bald eagle taught us about saving other endangered species? "I think there are lessons we can use, but they aren't simple lessons," says Deborah Jensen, Vice President and Director of Conservation Science and Stewardship for The Nature Conservancy.

First, "once decline was detected, people had to figure out why. That process can be used for any organism." The bald eagle might be nearing extinction today had we never discovered the connection between prolific use of DDT and nesting failure of eagles. Accurate population inventories and continuing scientific research are essential to detect problems, identify their causes, and develop solutions.

Designation of a species under the federal Endangered Species Act is vital. "It declares incontrovertibly that there is a problem," Jensen says. "Until that happens, then there is disagreement about whether or not a problem exists." Only with agreement come the resources and resolve necessary to remedy the problem.

Finally, says Jensen, "once a species is on the downward path, not all hope is lost. Recovery is possible. It will never be an easy fix, but that doesn't mean it isn't worth trying."

An early morning reflection in the Missouri River. STEVE JUSTAD

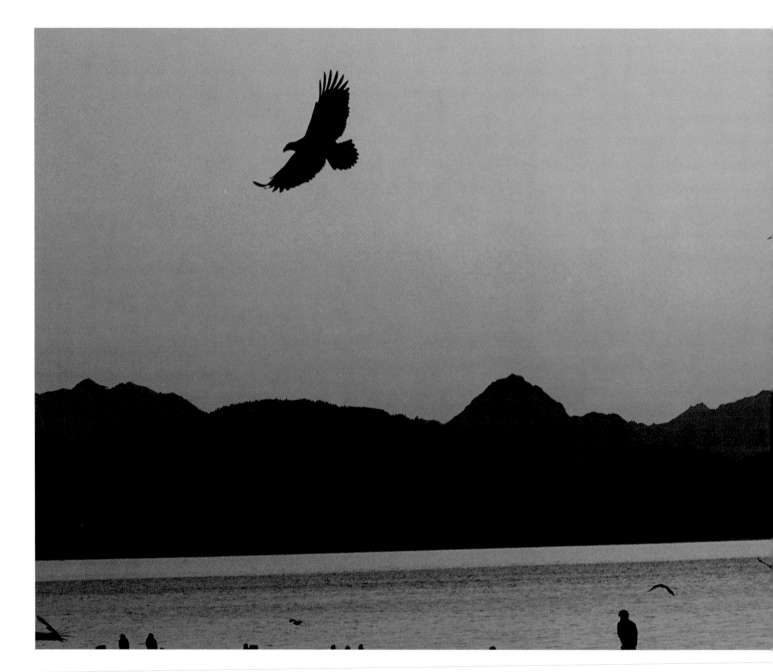

Heading back to roost at the close of another day. FRANK OBERLE

Hope inspires citizens to donate time, money, and effort. Hope produced the donations that set aside the James River National Wildlife Refuge. Hope drives National Wildlife Federation and Audubon volunteers into the cold and snow each winter to count wintering eagles. And it's hope that leads Jean Keene, a supervisor at a fish-packing plant who lives, quite literally, at the end of the road in Homer, Alaska, to set out fifty tons of freezer-burned fish for wintering birds. At times more than four hundred bald eagles gather behind her motor home. They occupy every available roost, and mill about with a rocking hunched-over gait, like stiff old men with wings, as they gulp down fish and the occasional intruding gull. "It gives them a helping hand during a tough time of the year," she says.

SCAVENGER AND FISH STEALER. Devoted mate for life, diligent parent, and hunter. We view our animals in moral terms. They are scoundrels or saints. Just as men create their gods, writes Barry Lopez in *Of Wolves and Men*, so do they also create their animals.

Not only does our severe anthropomorphism mislead us, it also blinds us to the eagle's exceptional adaptability. But if we insist on viewing the bald eagle in human terms, then I would offer this characterization from Stephen Fretwell in *The Bird Watch*. It hints at the complexity and utter suitability of the eagle to its environment. And Fretwell's remark, written as a fictional response of an eagle to a newspaper reporter, suggests also the reason the bald eagle is utterly suited to be our national symbol.

"The fellows who made me your symbol were more right than they knew," the eagle replies. "A fish dies and is washed up on shore. It looks bad and smells worse, is good for nothing, despised by all. I come and eat it and turn that fish … into a soaring wonder, a majestic greatness that stirs the heart of creatures everywhere, including men. Isn't that true for America, too? America was built by religious rejects, crooks, and poor people. All human waste, all looking bad and smelling worse, despised by all. This country consumed these people and … made them into a nation…. Like me, you … took the waste of the world and made something wonderful." ∽

Grace, power, and majesty. FRANK OBERLE

DIRECTORY OF BALD EAGLE VIEWING SITES

The following directory describes some of the best places to see wild bald eagles in the United States. Although eagles are likely to be seen at these areas during the recommended seasons, no sighting is guaranteed. Time and patience often are required to observe eagles, and many factors, including weather, influence the peak times of nesting, wintering, and migration. Eagle viewers should avoid disturbing birds, especially during nesting season. Maintain a reasonable distance, and use binoculars and spotting scopes for viewing.

ALABAMA

Lake Guntersville State Park

6,000-acre state park in NE Alabama. Best viewing: 50 to 60 bald eagles from Nov. through Feb., 80 to 100 at peak in Jan. Eagle Awareness Days in Jan.; activities include driving tours around lake. From US 431, take AL 227 E about 7 miles to park entrance. Signs posted from US 431 direct visitors to park. Contact: Lake Guntersville State Park Nature Center 256-571-5444.

Pickwick Lake

About 150 eagles congregate in severe winters (fewer when it's warm) where the Tennessee River meets Pickwick Lake, in NE Alabama near Tennessee and Mississippi. Peak time: mid-Dec. to mid-Feb. Best viewing: along a 7-mile stretch of the Tennessee River, where 40 eagles may regularly be seen. By car from Florence, take County 14 NE about 25 miles to Waterloo. By boat, float from the Riverton area to the Natchez Trace Bridge. Eagles may also be seen from County 14, which

follows the river for 2 miles before Waterloo. Land around Tennessee River owned by Tennessee Valley Authority. Contact: Alabama Nongame Wildlife Program 256-353-2634.

ALASKA

Alaska Chilkat Bald Eagle Preserve

48,000 acres of river bottomland of the Chilkat, Kleheni, and Tsirku rivers and part of Chilkat Lake, NW of Juneau. The Chilkat Valley is home to at least 400 bald eagles year-round; 5 miles of open water on the Chilkat River allow eagles to fish when other waters are frozen. About 150 pairs nest in the preserve. From early Oct. to Feb., more than 3,000 eagles may be seen in a small area. Best viewing: from Haines Hwy., miles 18 to 24. Managed by the Alaska Div. of Parks and Outdoor Recreation with the assistance of the Alaska Chilkat Bald Eagle Preserve Advisory Council. Contact: Alaska Div. of Parks and Outdoor Recreation, Haines office 907-766-2292; American Bald Eagle Foundation in Haines 907-766-3094.

Steep Creek

Steep Creek flows from Heintzleman Ridge to Mendenhall Lake. Bald eagles concentrate along the lower mile of the creek (which flows through kettle ponds before reaching the lake) to feed on spawning cohos in Oct. and Nov. and often into Feb. Best viewing: from parking lot of the Mendenhall Glacier Visitor Center Observatory or from Glacier Spur Rd., which parallels creek. Contact: Tongass National Forest, Juneau Ranger District 907-586-8800.

Stikine Flats Wildlife Viewing Area

As many as 1,500 bald eagles gather to feed on spawning eulachon in late Mar. to mid-May at Stikine Flats, at the mouth of the Stikine River in the Stikine–LeConte Wilderness Area, NW of Ketchikan. Look for them in the tall cottonwoods along the lower river and around pools and mudflats. Access by floatplane or boat only. Viewing from boat or beaches. Contact: Tongass National Forest, Wrangell Ranger District 907-874-2323.

Alaska is believed to support a breeding population of at least 20,000 bald eagles. Probably half of that population is in coastal SE Alaska, where the birds are easy to see. Any time of the year, the Alaska Marine Highway ferry system and tour cruises along the coast provide visitors with good views of bald eagles. Driving the roads around Juneau, Ketchikan, Sitka, and Petersburg also offers opportunities to view eagles. Each community has its own nesting and year-round concentration of eagles, though the birds are most conspicuous during summer. Contact: U.S. Fish and Wildlife Service 907-586-7243, www.alaska.fws.gov.

Other areas in Alaska with large breeding populations are the Alaska Peninsula, Aleutian Islands, Bering Sea, Cook Inlet, interior Alaska, Kodiak and Afognak, and south-central Alaska. Most of these areas are not as accessible as the southeast coast, however, nor do they have as high a concentration of eagles.

ARIZONA

Becker Lake Wildlife Area

This 630-acre site (with a 100-acre lake) is located in east-central Arizona near New Mexico. Rimmed with cottonwood, piñon, and juniper, it regularly attracts a half dozen bald eagles from Dec. through Mar. From Springerville, take US 60/US 180 N 2.5 miles to entrance. Contact: Arizona Game and Fish Dept., Pinetop 928-367-4281.

Lake Mary

Both Upper and Lower Lake Mary, about 1,000 acres combined, provide good viewing of wintering bald eagles, with peaks of 50 to 60 some winters. Best viewing: Nov. through Feb. along the paved highway that goes around the lakes at a higher elevation. On I-17 from Flagstaff, take exit 339. Go SE on Lake Mary Rd. (Forest Hwy. 3) for 6 miles to Lower Lake Mary and 9 miles to Upper Lake Mary. Contact: Coconino National Forest, Mormon Lake Ranger District 928-774-1147.

Luna Lake

More than a dozen eagles overwinter on Luna Lake, tucked in the White Mountains in NE Arizona. A breeding pair has occupied a nest, beginning in late Jan., in recent years. Eagles eat fish and pick off waterfowl in W end of lake. Ospreys also use the area. Best viewing: at the boat launch parking lot on the S shore. From Alpine, take 180 E about 4 miles to Luna Lake Wildlife Area parking lot. Contact: Alpine Ranger District 928-339-4384.

Mormon Lake

Bald eagles usually winter at Arizona's largest natural lake (about 9 square miles) from Nov. through Apr.; counts reach 50 to 60 some winters. Best viewing: Nov. to Feb. at Dough Morrison Outlook, E side of lake. Or drive the paved road around Mormon Lake (Forest Rd. 90). From Flagstaff, on I-17 at exit 339, take Lake Mary Rd. (Forest Hwy. 3) SE for 21 miles to Mormon Lake. Forest Rd. 90 circles around W side of the lake and returns to Forest Hwy. 3. Contact: USDA Forest Service, Mormon Lake Ranger District 928-774-1147.

Nelson Reservoir

A half dozen bald eagles spend the winter at this reservoir located on the Coronado Trail in SE Arizona near New Mexico. Typically, they arrive in Nov. and begin to migrate north in Mar. or Apr. The marshy area at the upper end of the reservoir, good waterfowl habitat, also attracts eagles. From Springerville, take US 191 (old US 666) E toward Alpine 8 miles. Contact: Apache-Sitgreaves National Forest 928-333-4301.

ARKANSAS

Beaver Lake

Up to 300 bald eagles winter on this 31,700-acre impoundment in NW Arkansas, a "Great Lake of the White River." An eagle pair nests on the lake most years. Numbers peak in Jan. and Feb. Best viewing by boat (but by car, too) between Rocky Branch Park and Dam Site Park, N part of lake. From Little Rock, travel W I-40 to Alma, N on I-540 to Rogers, then E on AR 12 (or N on AR 62). Go to Beaver Dam on the White River to watch eagles pick off trout. Eagle tours for a fee in late Jan. Contact: U.S. Army Corps of Engineers 479-636-1210.

Lake Greeson/Pike County

About 30–40 eagles winter on Lake Greeson, a 7,260-acre lake along the Little Missouri River N of Murfreesboro. Best viewing: by boat in Jan. and Feb. From Little Rock, travel S on I-30 to the Arkadelphia exit. Go W on AR 8, then W on US 70. Contact: U.S. Army Corps of Engineers, Lake Greeson Field Office 870-285-2151.

CALIFORNIA

Cache Creek

Wintering bald eagles populate a 25-mile stretch of Cache Creek (near Clear Lake) mid-Nov. through Mar. As many as 40 eagles were counted one Jan.; the colder the weather, the greater the concentration. Breeding population of at least 2 pairs. Good viewing near the North Fork of Cache Creek or from CA 16 along the creek. Guided hikes along Redbud Trail available late Jan. to Feb.; reservations required. From Clearlake Oaks on CA 20 drive E 8 miles to entrance/parking area. Contact: Bureau of Land Management 707-468-4000.

Eagle Lake

Winter and breeding populations frequent this 28,000-acre lake in NE California. About 35 to 50 bald eagles stay Nov. through Mar. if the lake remains ice-free. Best viewing along 8 miles of CA 139 on the N shore of lake; also on S shore between CA 139 N 25 miles to Eagle Lake, or take County A-1 NW 16 miles to S part of lake. Contact: Lassen National Forest 530-257-4188.

Lake San Antonio

From Nov. through Mar., more than 40 bald eagles roost in the shoreline snags of this 17-mile-long lake located between Monterey and San Luis Obispo. Best viewing: Jan. to Feb. from the Eagle Tour boat (birding information and binoculars provided). Reservations required; fee. At N edge of King City on US 101 take Jolon Rd. (G-14) exit W for 24 miles. Turn right on Interlake Rd. for 12 miles, then right on San Antonio Rd. to the lake. Contact: Monterey County Parks Dept. 805-472-2311.

Lewiston Lake and Trinity River Hatchery

More than a dozen eagle pairs nest on Lewiston and Trinity reservoirs on the Trinity River in north-central California. Some eagles remain all year, feeding on spawning salmon and steelhead, as well as fish released from the hatchery below the Lewiston dam. Best viewing: by boat or at fish hatchery. From Redding take CA 299 W 37 miles. Turn at sign to Trinity Dam/Lewiston Lake. At junction about 5.5 miles down, continue straight to Lewiston Lake or bear right to hatchery. Contact: Shasta-Trinity National Forest, Weaverville Ranger Station 530-623-2121.

Lower Klamath National Wildlife Refuge

This 46,900-acre refuge on the Oregon border, 1 of 6 in the Klamath Basin National Wildlife Refuges Complex, harbors up to 500 bald eagles from Dec. into Mar. They feed on waterfowl and rodents. Good viewing along auto tour in refuge; look for eagles roosting in willows. From I-5 take US 97 N, then turn E on CA 161 for 9 miles to Lower Klamath auto tour. Contact: Klamath Basin National Wildlife Refuges Complex 530-667-2231.

Silverwood Lake State Recreation Area

About 10 bald eagles, mature and immature, winter Dec. through Mar. in this 2,400-acre state park NE of Los Angeles. Park rangers and volunteers offer eagle boat tours Jan. through mid-Mar.; reservations required. Visitors may participate in midwinter eagle counts. In Cajon Pass area on I-15 take CA 138 E for 12 miles to lake. Contact: California State Parks 760-389-2303.

COLORADO

Alamosa, Monte Vista, and Baca National Wildlife Refuges

Three national wildlife refuges make up this 14,189-acre complex in south-central Colorado near New Mexico. Staging bald eagles arrive during spring thaw around mid-Mar.; 40 to 100 eagles feed on exposed winter-killed fish on the Rio Grande. Good viewing from self-guided auto tour. Take US 160 E of Alamosa 3 miles or El Rancho Ln. S of Alamosa 2 miles. Contact: Alamosa National Wildlife Refuge 719-589-4021.

Barr Lake State Park

A single pair of bald eagles has nested and remained year-round in this 2,715-acre park NE of Denver. 10 to 20 eagles show up from Nov. through Mar. Numbers peak in Jan. Birds can usually be viewed from hiking trails. Stop at nature center for viewing information. Nearest town is Brighton. Take I-76 E of Denver to exit 22, Bromley Ln. Go E on Bromley for 0.75 mile to Picadilly Rd. Turn right for 1.5 miles to park entrance; continue to nature center. Contact: Barr Lake State Park 303-659-6005.

Colorado River

Wintering bald eagles are often seen along US 550 between Montrose and Ouray and along the Colorado River, especially along Trough Rd. between Kremmling and State Bridge.

Jackson Lake State Park

Jackson Lake is a major stopover for migrant bald eagles Feb. through April and Sept. through Oct. Good roadside viewing in and around park; look for eagles in cottonwoods near water. Between Jackson Lake and Denver, 48 pairs nest along the South Platte. Take I-76 NE of Denver, or US 34 E; signed exits lead to park. Contact: Jackson Lake State Park 970-645-2551.

Rocky Mountain Arsenal National Wildlife Refuge

A 27-square-mile area just outside Denver, with 3,600 acres designated as the Rocky Mountain Arsenal Bald Eagle Management Area. From Nov. to Feb., a major winter roost on the E side of the wildlife area attracts 32 eagles that feed mostly on prairie dogs. The Eagle Watch, an observation point, overlooks the roost. Programs scheduled for visitors. To the Eagle Watch, take the Chambers Rd. exit N from I-70 to 56th St. Travel E on 56th to Buckley Rd. for 1.5 miles. Contact: Rocky Mountain Arsenal National Wildlife Refuge 303-289-0232.

CONNECTICUT

Connecticut River

Private companies offer guided boat tours on the Connecticut River for winter bald eagle viewing. The 100-foot *Sunbeam Express* offers a bald eagle tour in Feb. and Mar. Contact: Sunbeam Fleet 860-443-7259.

Shepaug Eagle Observation Area

Up to 20 bald eagles winter near the open water of Shepaug Reservoir and dam on the Housatonic River, NE of Danbury. Reservations required; begin making them in mid-Dec. for weekends and Wednesdays throughout the winter. Guided viewing from blind with telescopes. Contact: Northeast Utilities 800-368-8954.

DELAWARE

Bombay Hook National Wildlife Refuge

On Delaware's Atlantic coast, a 15,978-acre refuge with 1 nesting pair of bald eagles year-round and some migrating immature birds. Best viewing: Nov. through Mar., when nest trees are bare, along Shearness Rd. along Shearness Pool. Group tours available. Coming S on US 13, drive toward Smyrna. At the third stoplight in Smyrna, turn left onto Rd. 12. This will turn into DE 9. Drive S 0.25 miles more to sign for refuge. Turn left onto Rd. 85 and continue to visitor center. Contact: Bombay Hook National Wildlife Refuge 302-653-6872.

FLORIDA

Big Bend Wildlife Management Area: Hickory Mound Impoundment

A 6.5-mile dike encircles this 1,834-acre management area SE of Tallahassee on the Gulf coast. Bald eagles stay here year-round, with largest concentrations during fall migration Sept. through Oct. One active nest on Hickory Mound Impoundment and several in Taylor County; birds nest in Feb. and Mar. View of Impoundment nest from observation tower. On US 98, 18 miles W of Perry, turn W on Cow Creek Grade. Drive 6 miles on limerock road to check station for map and regulations summary. Contact: Big Bend Wildlife Management Area Field Office 850-838-9016.

Lake Kissimmee State Park

Bald eagles can be seen year-around, and several pairs nest in this 5,800-acre park in central Florida, E of Tampa. Best viewing: Nov. through Mar. Look for eagles from 13 miles of hiking trails or from the observation tower. From US 27 in Lake Wales, take FL 60 E 10 miles to Boy Scout Rd. Turn left for 3.7 miles. Turn right onto Camp Mack Rd. for 5.6 miles to park entrance. Contact: Dept. of Environmental Protection 863-696-1112.

Merritt Island National Wildlife Refuge

This 140,000-acre island on Florida's E coast shares a common boundary with Kennedy Space Center and Canaveral National Seashore. Bald eagles present late Sept. through Mar.; nesting begins late Nov. Numbers of pairs and individuals vary according to weather; few remain year-round. Good viewing along Black Point Wildlife Drive by car; also, from observation tower, photo blind, and trails within the park. The visitor information center is located on SR 402 5 miles E of U.S. 1 in Titusville. Contact: Merritt Island National Wildlife Refuge 321-861-0667.

Three Lakes Wildlife Management Area: Prairie Lakes Unit

Prairie Lakes S of Orlando, nearly 9,000 acres of former ranch land, with about a dozen active nests during winter nesting season, mid-Oct. through mid-May. Many eagles remain year-round. During nesting season some restrictions apply; please observe posted area around nests. (Endangered red-cockaded woodpeckers also nest here.) Good viewing from 5-mile hiking loop of the Florida Trail, or driving on Canoe Creek Rd. (FL 523). Boardwalk near Lake Marian and an observation tower on Lake Jackson. From Kenansville drive 9 miles NW on Canoe Creek Rd. Entrance on left (W). Contact: Florida Fish and Wildlife Conservation Commission 407-436-1818.

GEORGIA

Ansley Hodges M.A.R.S.H. Project

A waterfowl impoundment constructed with help from Ducks Unlimited on Altamaha Wildlife Management Area, a coastal marsh system. Many waterfowl and shorebirds, as well as bald eagles, especially in winter and spring. Take Exit 49 on I-95 at the junction of I-95 and SR 251 (Briardam Road). Travel E on SR 251 to the junction of SR 251 and US 17. Turn S on US 17 and continue through Darien. The entrance to Ansley Hodges will be 3.5 miles on the right. Contact: Altamaha Wildlife Management Area 912-262-3173.

Jekyll Island

Georgia's breeding population of bald eagles has been increasing. Most eagles are found along the coast and barrier islands. Unfortunately, many places don't provide public viewing areas. One area where eagles are visible is Jekyll Island, a coastal island on Colonial Coast Birding Trail. Contact: Jekyll Island Welcome Center 912-635-3636.

IDAHO

Dworshak Reservoir

5 active nests ring Dworshak Reservoir on the Clearwater River. 20–50 eagles visit Nov. through Feb. Concentrations are greatest when the dam is spilling water. Best viewing: along Ahsahka Rd. (road to powerhouse, which goes to base of dam). Walking trail along other side of dam. Near Orofino in N Idaho, at lower end of panhandle. From Orofino, cross Orofino Bridge and turn left on ID 7. Turn right just before Ahsahka Bridge and follow A Road to dam. Contact: U.S. Army Corps of Engineers Visitor Center 208-476-1255.

Lake Coeur d'Alene/Wolf Lodge Bay

The 900-acre bay attracts up to 60 migratory bald eagles when the kokanee salmon begin to spawn in Nov. Population peaks late Dec. to early Jan. Viewing from boat or car. Detailed brochure available. 8 miles E of Coeur d'Alene on I-90 and take Wolf Lodge exit. Turn right and follow State Hwy. 97 to boat launch and Mineral Ridge Trailhead. Contact: Bureau of Land Management 208-769-5000.

Silver Creek Preserve

In this 900-acre preserve 35 miles SE of Sun Valley, about a dozen wintering bald eagles perch in trees and feed on waterfowl and fish in the creek's open spring-fed water. Good viewing Nov. to Feb. Walk or cross-country ski to area of large cottonwoods overlooking Sullivan's Lake. Directly off ID 20, 2 miles W of Picabo. Park and sign in at visitor center. Contact: The Nature Conservancy 208-788-7910.

South Fork Snake River

The South Fork valley produces most of Idaho's bald eagles and has a large year-round population. Up to 200 birds winter here. Best viewing: in summer, by boat. Contact: Bureau of Land Management, Idaho Falls District 208-524-7500.

ILLINOIS

Cedar Glenn Eagle Roost

During cold winters, more than 400 bald eagles loiter among the 1,680 acres of varied habitat along the Mississippi River in W Illinois on the Iowa-Missouri border. Peak viewing: Jan. and Feb., from areas near the preserve. (See Keokuk, IA, in this directory.) Closed to the public Nov. 1 to Mar. 1 for protection of the wintering eagles. The main road and bridge is IL 136. From the Illinois end of the bridge follow IL 136 E toward Hamilton. After 0.25 miles, turn S at the sign for Warsaw. The highway is not numbered but is part of the Great River Road. Contact: Western Illinois University Kibbe Life Science Research Station resident manager 217-256-4519.

Crab Orchard National Wildlife Refuge

43,890 acres in S Illinois, near Carbondale. Dec. to Mar. viewing of about 20 bald eagles peaks in Jan.; 6 nesting pairs year-round. Viewing possible from Crab Orchard Lake. Van tours leave from interpretive center to restricted areas. Sign up early. Eagle weekends in late Jan. From I-57 exit 54b, 7 miles W on IL 13. Contact: Crab Orchard National Wildlife Refuge 618-997-3344.

Lock and Dam 15/Quad Cities

Up to 100 wintering bald eagles flock to the open water around the lock and dam on the Mississippi River at Rock Island and Moline, Illinois, and Davenport and Bettendorf, Iowa, collectively known as the Quad Cities. Best viewing: Dec. through Feb. from Fisherman's Corner Public Use Area, S entrance; Davenport riverfront, downstream of dam; Rock

Island riverfront, downstream of dam; and Credit Island. Quad Cities Bald Eagle Days feature environmental exhibits, wildlife art, and eagle watching. Corps of Engineers park ranger leads eagle-watching weekends in Jan. Contact: Mississippi River Visitor Center (on Arsenal Island) 309-794-5338.

INDIANA

Monroe Lake

Bald eagles loiter year-around on Monroe Lake in S Indiana. 3 to 4 pairs nest late Feb. through early summer. Up to 40 bald eagles (and even some migrating goldens) show up in winter. Best winter watching: Jan. and Feb. when break up unlocks dead shad frozen in lake ice. Best views are from overlook areas around lake, boat launching area, or boat. One- to two-day eagle education program in Feb.; sign up early. Drive E from Bloomington on IN 46 and S on IN 446 about 6 miles to Paynetown Visitor Center. Contact: Indiana Dept. of Natural Resources 812-837-9546.

Patoka Lake

Several nesting pairs and up to 20 wintering eagles frequent Patoka Lake, 25 miles long with 161 miles of shoreline, in south-central Indiana. Best viewing: Fisherman's Campground, upper beach parking lot, Newton-Stewart Ramp, marina, South Ramp, and Hwy. 145. Visitor center has printed material on local eagle viewing. Programs and special events. Captive eagle at visitors center. From Jasper, turn N off IN 164 at Wicklife. Follow this road past gatehouse to visitor center. Contact: Indiana Dept. of Natural Resources Patoka Lake Visitor Center 812-685-2447.

IOWA

Lake Red Rock

20 to 40 eagles gather Dec. through mid-Mar. below the dam forming Lake Red Rock on the Des Moines River, SE of Des Moines. Numbers peak in late Dec. and early Jan. Winter viewing along river, near campground, and from bike trail. From Pella, take T-15 S for 4 miles to Red Rock Dam. Contact: U.S. Army Corps of Engineers Visitor Center (at S end of dam) 641-828-7522.

Lock and Dam 19/Keokuk

From Nov. to Mar., up to 400 wintering bald eagles congregate in the largest area of open water on the Mississippi River below Lock and Dam 19 at Keokuk, where Iowa, Illinois, and Missouri meet. Numbers peak in Jan. Bald Eagle Appreciation Days in Jan.; indoor and outdoor activities. River City Mall displays. Eagle watching at the dam. Contact: Keokuk Area Convention & Tourism Bureau 800-383-1219.

See also Lock and Dam 15/Quad Cities in Illinois listings.

KANSAS

John Redmond Dam and Reservoir

The reservoir, with a 59-mile shoreline, lies in a broad valley in the Flint Hills region S of Topeka. About 50 wintering bald eagles Oct. through Mar., with numbers peaking in Jan. and Feb. Best viewing: from upstream side of dam and around shoreline, Riverside West Park below dam, also from town of Ottumwo at Hickory Creek. All areas accessible by car. Walking trail and observation tower at Doves Roost (W of Kennedy Creek, N side of lake). On the Neosho River about 3 miles N and 1 mile W of Burlington, just off US 75. Contact: U.S. Army Corps of Engineers 620-364-8613. The local Audubon chapter in conjunction with the Flint Hills National Wildlife Refuge sponsors an Eagle Tour in Jan.; call the refuge headquarters at 620-392-5553 in Dec. for dates.

Perry Reservoir

Wintering bald eagles can be seen Nov. through early Mar. around this 11,500-acre lake, with up to 200 birds in Jan. Most viewing from car. From Topeka, drive E on US 24 about

15 miles. Turn N at Perry for 3 miles. Owner: U.S. Army Corps of Engineers. Contact: Perry Reservoir Information Center 785-597-5144.

SpringHill Suites, Lawrence

One-way glass in a public viewing area in SpringHill Suites looks out over wintering area on the Kansas River, where 10 to 20 eagles gather Dec. to Feb. Eagle rooms for rent for close-up views through ceiling-to-floor windows. Take I-70 to exit 204 (E Lawrence). Travel S 1 mile over bridge, turn left and drive one block to corner of 6th and New Hampshire. Contact: SpringHill Suites by Marriott 785-841-2700.

KENTUCKY

Ballard Wildlife Management Area

Several bald eagle pairs nest on Ballard, 8,024 acres including 11 oxbow lakes, in W Kentucky. Viewing from 1-mile loop in car or on foot. From Paducah, travel US 60 W 17 miles to LaCenter. Take KY 358 for 5.6 miles to KY 473 into Bandana. Take KY 1105 6 miles to KY 473 again. Turn left off 473 at Lodge Rd. for 1 mile to entrance. Contact: Kentucky Dept. of Fish and Wildlife Resources 800-858-1549.

Land Between the Lakes

See Land Between the Lakes in Tennessee section. To N entrance: From I-24, go 5 miles S on KY 453 through Grand Rivers.

LOUISIANA

White Kitchen Preserve

A freshwater marsh and cypress swamp preserve. Sept. through May, a single nesting pair of bald eagles at site that has been occupied for at least 80 to 90 years (even surviving a direct hit from Hurricane Katrina). Site visible from the end of the Chevron Boardwalk. Best viewing: Feb. and Mar. Self-guided tour brochure available at local stores and restaurants or from Louisiana Field Office of the Nature Conservancy. The short boardwalk begins at State of Louisiana rest area at junction of US 190 and US 90 near southern Louisiana-Mississippi border. Contact: The Nature Conservancy 985-809-1414.

MAINE

Acadia National Park

This 47,748-acre national park S of Bangor, with both inland and coastal habitat, harbors bald eagles year-round. Several nesting pairs arrive late Feb. and Mar. and fledge in early July. Best viewing: June through Aug. with private water-based tours often accompanied by naturalists. Park visitor center open May 1 to Oct. 31. A smaller winter visitor center is open year-around. Take ME 3 to Mt. Desert Island and follow signs. Park headquarters, off ME 233, open in winter. Contact: Acadia National Park 207-288-3338.

Cobscook Bay State Park/Moosehorn National Wildlife Refuge

The national wildlife refuge, of which the state park is a part, is located on Cobscook Bay on Maine's northernmost coast. It boasts the Northeast's highest density of nesting bald eagles. Dozens remain year-round. Several nesting pairs visible Mar. through Aug., with some pairs right on the bay. Magurrewock Marsh in Baring Unit of refuge also a good spot for viewing. To reach the state park take US 1 E from Machias through Whiting. Signs for park posted on E side of 1. Contact: 207-726-4412. For refuge, take ME 9 to US 1 through Baring to entrance on S side of 1. Contact: Moosehorn National Wildlife Refuge 207-454-7161.

Holbrook Island Sanctuary

This 1,250-acre state park W of Acadia National Park includes both freshwater ponds and saltwater shoreline. Pairs of mature bald eagles year-round, with a few nesting sites in the park or nearby. Viewing from car and from trails, some along shoreline. Day use only. From ME 176 look for Cape Rosier Rd. on W side. Follow signs to park. Contact: Maine Bureau of Parks and Land 207-326-4012.

Kennebec River

Increasing numbers of eagles have nested along the Kennebec River between Augusta and Waterville and loiter in the area through summer. Best access by boat or canoe. Float Sidney to Waterville for half-day canoe trip. Longer trip: Waterville to Augusta. Route 104 runs along W shore of river. Contact: Maine Dept. of Inland Fisheries and Wildlife 207-287-8000.

Steve Powell Wildlife Management Area/Swan Island

A bald eagle pair nests on one of the two islands making up this 1,755-acre management area on the Kennebec River between Augusta and Brunswick. Several other pairs nest nearby. Best viewing: early May through Labor Day along the Kennebec and on islands, by canoe or on trails; reservations required. Interpretative tours available. Parking area and boat landing in Richmond on riverbank. Contact: Maine Dept. of Inland Fisheries and Wildlife 207-547-5319.

The Nature Conservancy in Maine owns 20 preserves protecting the bald eagle habitat in Maine. These sites are protected by the Nature Conservancy in part because the eagles are particularly sensitive to disturbance. The sites are not open to the public during the nesting season. The Nature Conservancy's Maine Chapter is also involved in cooperative bald eagle protection projects with such groups as the U.S. Fish and Wildlife Service, Maine Dept. of Inland Fisheries and Wildlife, and Land for Maine's Future Board.

MARYLAND

Barton Cove

A single nesting pair of bald eagles occupies Barton Island, in the Connecticut River N of Northampton, from Feb. through July. Best viewing: from public boat ramp off MA 2, or just E of boat ramp at Barton Cove Nature and Camping Area. Boating prohibited in immediate area surrounding Barton Island and nest. Both boat ramp and nature area in Gill just off MA 2. From I-91, follow MA 2 E through Greenfield through first stoplight in Gill. Follow signs for boat ramp. Contact: Northfield Mountain Recreation and Environmental Center 413-659-3714 or 800-859-2960.

Blackwater National Wildlife Refuge

About 20 nesting pairs and often more than 100 wintering eagles frequent the refuge, more than 20,000 acres 12 miles S of Cambridge on the Eastern Shore, Chesapeake Bay. (An occasional golden eagle shows up.) Drive, walk, or bike self-guided tour on the wildlife drive for views of eagles in tall loblolly pines; get tour brochure at visitor center. Contact: Blackwater National Wildlife Refuge 410-228-2677.

Other eagle concentration areas on Chesapeake Bay include Aberdeen Proving Grounds, Caledon State Park, Mason Neck National Wildlife Refuge, and the towns of Pocomoke, Hopewell, and Rappahannock. Contact: U.S. Fish and Wildlife Service in Annapolis 410-228-2692.

Conowingo Dam

From mid-Nov. through Jan., up to 40 bald eagles congregate around the open water of the Lower Susquehanna River above and below Conowingo Dam. Peak numbers of eagles in Dec. Nesting pairs in Conowingo Recreation Project area; some migrants in Aug. Viewing platform at Conowingo Fishermen's Park and Boat Launch below dam, about 0.5 miles from parking area. On US 1 just S of Pennsylvania in NE Maryland. Contact: Conowingo Hydroelectric Station 410-457-5011.

MASSACHUSETTS

Quabbin Reservoir

Up to 50 wintering eagles and more than a half dozen breeding pairs use this 25,000-acre impoundment E of

Northampton. Peak viewing in Feb. from Endfield Lookout. Off MA 9 between Ware and Belchertown. Contact: Dept. of Conservation and Recreation, Quabbin Visitor Center 413-323-7221.

MICHIGAN

Erie Marsh

Migrating bald eagles can be seen in this preserve, one of many marshes along Lake Erie in SE Michigan. Best viewing: Mar. through Apr. and early fall, from trails throughout preserve; watch for roosting and flying eagles. Closed for duck hunting mid-Sept. through Nov. From Monroe take I-75 S to exit 2 (Summit Rd.). Go SE on Summit to Stearns Rd. Make a U-turn and head back N/NE on Bay Creek Rd. 0.8 mile to Dean Rd. Turn E on Dean Creek for 1 mile. Park at the Erie Shooting Club Cottages. Contact: The Nature Conservancy, Michigan Field Office 517-316-0300.

Presque Isle Flowage

More than 50 bald eagle pairs nest in Ottawa National Forest in the western Upper Peninsula. Some remain during winter by feeding on road-killed white-tailed deer. Eagles can be seen on every lake larger than about 200 acres. About 2.5 miles S of Marenisco on MI 64. Entrance W side of road. Contact: Ottawa National Forest 906-667-0261.

Seney National Wildlife Refuge

Several bald eagle pairs nest and many immature eagles summer on this 95,455-acre wildlife refuge in the middle of the Upper Peninsula, in Schoolcraft County. Best viewing: Feb. to late Oct., when ice forms, from 7-mile Marshland Wildlife Drive self-guided tour. Eagle nest observation deck with spotting scope and interpretive panel located along drive. Visitor center open May 15 to Oct. 15. 3 entry points to refuge: entrance road off MI 77, 2 miles N of Germfask; Driggs River Rd. off MI 28; and at cross-country ski area off MI 77, S of Germfask. Contact: Seney National Wildlife Refuge 906-586-9851.

MINNESOTA

Chippewa National Forest

More than 150 breeding pairs frequent this 1.6 million-acre forest (41 percent federally owned), with 1,300 lakes and ponds, 925 miles of streams, and 400,000 acres of wetlands. Best viewing: mid-Mar. through Nov. by canoe on Mississippi River between Cass Lake and Lake Winnie (or from car on US 2); also by Federal Dam at Leech Lake, Winnie Dam at the E end of Lake Winnibigoshish, Knutson Dam on Cass Lake, and other large lakes and streams. View from boat, walking along shores, and at campgrounds, picnic areas, and boat landings. Educational programs at various forest visitor centers. Contact: Chippewa National Forest 218-335-8600.

Lac qui Parle Wildlife Management Area

During Nov. and Dec., dozens of bald eagles follow migrating waterfowl into this 33,000-acre refuge and management area near Milan in Chippewa County. Both waterfowl and eagles remain during mild winters. About a half dozen pairs nest in the area. Occasional golden eagle in the fall. Best viewing: along County 32 N 1 mile from County 13, and from other roads near Lac qui Parle Lake. Contact: Lac qui Parle Wildlife Management Area 320-734-4451.

Mississippi River at Red Wing

The Mississippi River south of the Twin Cities is a haven for wintering eagles. From Nov. through Mar., Colvill Park and Bay Point Park in Red Wing, 55 miles SE of the Twin Cities, attract concentrations. Numbers peak in Dec. Follow MN 61 W to Red Wing. Watch for signs to waterfront parks. Eagle Watch Weekend mid-Feb. at Colvill Park. Contact: Red Wing Visitor and Convention Bureau 800-498-3444 or visitorscenter@redwing.org.

Mississippi River near Wabasha-Winona

About three dozen bald eagle pairs nest in the Winona District of the Upper Mississippi National Wildlife and Fish Refuge (see also Wisconsin). From Nov. to Mar., 50 to 75 bald eagles feed at Wabasha, about 115 miles SE of the Twin Cities, where the Chippewa River flows into the Mississippi and creates ice-free water all winter. Best viewing: riverside viewing platforms at the National Eagle Center in Wabasha, and from road pull-outs between Camp Lacupolis and Read's Landing. Contact: National Eagle Center 651-565-4989 or 877-332-4537.

Sherburne National Wildlife Refuge

This refuge on the Saint Francis River just NW of the Twin Cities is year-round habitat for some bald eagles. Recently 8 nesting pairs Apr. to Aug. Some winter nearby below warm-water discharge from nuclear plant on Mississippi near Monticello. Peak viewing of nesting pairs May to June from observation decks with telescopes located along 8-mile wildlife drive. Visitor centers offer educational programs for groups. From I-94, take MN 101 from Rogers to Elk River, where road becomes US 169. Go N on 169 about 20 miles, then W on County 9 for 4 miles to entrance. Contact: Sherburne National Wildlife Refuge 763-389-3323.

Tamarac National Wildlife Refuge

Two dozen pairs nest on this 43,000-acre refuge E of Fargo, North Dakota, and additional eagles nest nearby. During mild winters, a few eagles remain year-round with high numbers in spring and summer, peaking at about 100 during migration in Oct. and Nov. Best viewing: from County 26 on refuge boundary, on walking trails within refuge near water, and from auto tour route. Located 18 miles NW of Detroit Lakes off County 29 and 26. Contact: Tamarac National Wildlife Refuge Visitor Center 218-847-2641.

Voyageurs National Park

About 30 bald eagle pairs nest in Voyageurs National Park, where lakes large and small make up nearly 40 percent of the park's total area. Best viewing: shorelines and islands of large lakes such as Rainy, Kabetogama, and Namakan. Eagles remain year-round, fishing in open water and feeding off roadkill and wolf kills. In spring, when ice breaks up in Black Bay near Rainy Lake, as many as 120 eagles feed on fish. Best viewing: from boat; guided tours offered. Leave car at visitor centers. Naturalist-guided programs. To Rainy Lake, drive 12 miles E of International Falls on MN 11. To Kabetogama Lake, take US 53, then MN 122 4 miles to visitor center. Contact: Voyageurs National Park 218-283-9821.

MISSISSIPPI

Arkabutla Lake

Nesting and wintering eagles use Arkabutla Lake, one of four flood-reduction reservoirs in N Mississippi. The lake totals about 20,000 acres; the project includes an additional 37,700 acres of public land. 7 boat-launching ramps. I-55 to Hernando (exit 280) or Coldwater (exit 271). Arkabutla Dam is on Scenic Loop 304. Contact: U.S. Army Corps of Engineers 662-562-6261.

Grenada Lake

35,000-acre Grenada Lake is another of the large impoundments in northern Mississippi, constructed to help control flooding along the Yazoo River Basin. The reservoir, with a shoreline of about 150 miles, is surrounded by 55,000 acres of public land. Both nesting and wintering bald eagles frequent the lake. 16 boat ramps, 25 recreation areas, 4 hiking trails. I-55 to exit 206, Highway 8 E for approximately 4 miles, follow 333 scenic loop drive to dam. Contact: U.S. Army Corps of Engineers 662-226-5911.

Sardis Lake

Nesting and wintering bald eagles are also found on Sardis Lake, a 98,500-acre reservoir on the Little Tallahatchie River in N Mississippi. Nature trails, auto-accessible viewing areas, 10 boat ramps. I-55 to Sardis (exit 252), go 10 miles E on

MS 315 to Sardis Dam. Or I-55 to Batesville (exit 246), go 10 miles E on MS 35 to Sardis Dam. Contact: U.S. Army Corps of Engineers 662-563-4531.

Eagles are also common along Mississippi's Gulf Coast. Two good areas to check out: Grand Bay National Wildlife Refuge, about 10 miles E of Pascagoula on Bayou Heron Road 228-475-0765; and Gulf Island National Seashore, I-10 exit 57 or 50 to US Highway 90 to Ocean Springs 228-875-9057.

MISSOURI

Eagle Days

The Missouri Dept. of Conservation hosts Eagle Days, a series of events in Dec. and Jan. at various locations. Activities include indoor educational programs with a live bald eagle and guided outdoor viewing. Contact: Missouri Dept. of Conservation 573-522-4115, ext. 3289, or www.mdc.mo.gov/events/eagledays.

Sandy Island Natural History Area

Up to 200 eagles winter in the 28-acre Sandy Island Eagle Sanctuary near Lock and Dam 25 (Winfield Dam) on the Mississippi River. The area was donated by Missouri photographer Frank Oberle (chief photographer of this book) and his wife, Judy, in 1992 as safe habitat for bald eagles. Nearby, the Mary Wiese Observation Platform is located on Corps of Engineers property at the S end of lock and dam. Off MO 79 about 40 minutes N of St. Louis. Contact: The Nature Conservancy 314-968-1105 or 573-323-8790; U.S. Army Corps of Engineers 304-586-3445.

MONTANA

Fort Peck Dam

40 or more wintering bald eagles congregate on open water below the Fort Peck Dam in NE Montana from Nov. to Mar. Best viewing: near dam at the Fort Peck Interpretive Center and from gravel and dirt roads below power plants. Off Mt 117 (Lower Yellowstone Rd.) below Fort Peck power plants. Contact: U.S. Army Corps of Engineers 406-526-3493.

Gates of the Mountains

On Holter Lake; boat access only. About a half dozen nesting pairs, and a total of two dozen adult and immature birds in the summer. Additional migrating birds in the fall. Gates of the Mountains boat tour offers 2-hour cruise for fee. Private boats pay launch fee. Private visitor center at boat launch. From Helena drive 20 miles N on I-15 to Gates of the Mountains exit. Continue 2.8 miles to boat tour and public boat launch. Contact: Gates of the Mountains 406-458-5241.

Kootenai River/Libby Dam

About a half dozen pairs nest within 5 miles of the dam. (Check the eagle cam at www.libbymt.com/webcam/libby-dameaglecam.htm from May to mid-July, when nesting eagles are most active.) 25 to over 100 bald eagles winter below Libby Dam on the Kootenai River in NW Montana. Numbers peak Dec. through Jan. Best viewing: from roads along the river and from Alexander Creek Picnic Area. Visitor center on Forest Service Rd. 228. From Libby go N on MT 37 13.5 miles to FSR 228. Turn W, go about 3.5 miles to the visitor center. Contact: U.S. Army Corps of Engineers 406-293-5577.

Lee Metcalf National Wildlife Refuge

Up to 20 bald eagles frequent this site on the Bitterroot River, winter through Mar. Picnic area, 140 acres, open year-round for walking and wildlife viewing. Take US 93 to Stevensville. Turn E on Eastside Hwy. Turn on Wildfowl Ln. for 1.5 miles; watch for refuge boundary signs. Contact: Lee Metcalf National Wildlife Refuge 406-777-5552.

Rocky Mountain Front

More than 100 bald eagles migrate through this area on the eastern front of the Rocky Mountains mid-Feb. to mid-Apr., with highest numbers in Mar. (Numbers even higher for golden eagles.) Best viewing: from Bowmans Corners to Rogers Pass; find vantage point along MT 200. From Lincoln, go E on MT 200 15 miles to top of Rogers Pass, or hike up the Continental Divide Trail. Continue E to Bowmans Corners at junction of 200 and US 287. Contact: USDA Forest Service, Helena National Forest 406-362-4265.

NEBRASKA

Johnson 2 Hydro Plant

From mid-Dec. to Mar., a dozen or more bald eagles congregate on the open water near this hydro plant on the Tri-County Supply Canal in south-central Nebraska. (Numbers were higher before drought restricted water releases.) Plant provides spotting scopes and bleachers at viewing windows. From I-80 take Lexington exit S onto US 283. Past truck stop, go left on blacktop canyon road for 3 miles S, 1 mile E, and 1 mile S again over supply canal. Turn W (right) onto unmarked county road and continue to plant. Contact: Central Nebraska Public Power and Irrigation District 308-995-8601.

Kingsley Dam

A couple dozen wintering eagles gather below the dam at Lake Ogallala to feast on dead fish. (Drought has reduced the number of eagles.) Water stays open when nearby waters freeze. Mid-Dec. through Mar.; numbers peak Jan. through Feb. Small heated trailer with large bay windows available for viewing. From I-80, exit at Ogallala. Go N through town and follow signs for Lake McConaughy and Kingsley Dam. Contact: Central Nebraska Public Power and Irrigation District 308-284-2332.

NEVADA

Eagles in Agriculture

Bald eagles, ever the opportunists, pour into the Carson Valley in northern Nevada during calving season to clean up the messy remains of birthing. During the Eagles and Agriculture Event in late Feb. birdwatchers can tour area ranches and Nature Conservancy land to watch the birds at work. Contact: Carson Valley Visitors Authority 800-727-7677, TNC Field Office 775-322-4990, and Lahontan Audubon Society 775-324-2473.

Lahontan State Recreation Area

Upper and Lower Lahontan Reservoirs, 17 miles long with a total of 69 miles of shoreline, are located on Carson River. A half dozen wintering bald eagles may be seen Nov. through Mar. View by driving or walking around lake. Look in trees along shoreline. Located 50 miles E of Carson City off NV 50 or 20 miles SW of Fallon off NV 50. Contact: Nevada Div. of State Parks 775-867-3500.

Lake Mead National Recreation Area

Nearly 100 bald eagles winter late Nov. through Apr. on this 1.5 million-acre recreation area, which comprises Lake Mead, formed by Hoover Dam; Lake Mohave, formed behind Davis Dam; and the land surrounding these lakes. Best viewing is by boating on either lake, specifically the Cottonwood Grove area on Lake Mohave and the Overton Arm on Lake Mead; also, driving the Northshore Rd. within the recreation area. Located in the southern tip of Nevada, 25 miles SE of Las Vegas. Access off US 93-95 from Las Vegas or off I-15 at the N end of the recreation area. Contact: Alan Bible Visitor Center 702-293-8990.

Ruby Lake National Wildlife Refuge

Up to 4 eagles winter on this 39,926-acre refuge system of marshes Nov. through Feb. A single eagle often perches in a large tree near the historic site of Bressman Cabin on County 767. More viewing from diked roads throughout marsh system. Golden eagles are also seen. From Elko take Jiggs Hwy. (NV 228). Travel 3 miles beyond Jiggs and turn left onto Harrison Pass Summit Rd. Turn right onto County 767, also called Ruby Lake Valley Rd. This road sometimes closes in winter; call ahead for information. The refuge headquarters is 9 miles down this road. Contact: Ruby Lake National Wildlife Refuge 775-779-2237.

Stillwater National Wildlife Refuge

Up to 10 bald eagles winter late Nov. through Mar. on this 77,000-acre refuge. Drive roads throughout refuge and look for eagles near units that have open water. Located 15 miles E of Fallon off NV 50. Contact: Stillwater National Wildlife Refuge 775-428-6452.

NEW HAMPSHIRE

Adam's Point Wildlife Management Area

5 to 15 bald eagles winter in these 4,500 acres of tidal water and wetlands and 800 acres of coastal land in New Hampshire's Great Bay area. Best viewing: late Nov. through Mar., from walking trail leading onto point; look for eagles along open water. Access trail from University of New Hampshire Jackson Lab parking lot. From Durham, take NH 108 toward Newmarket; after Oyster River, take first left on Durham Point Rd. about 3 miles to fence and sign for lab; road to parking lot through opening in fence. Contact: New Hampshire Fish and Game 603-271-2461, Audubon Society of New Hampshire 603-224-9909.

Bald eagles winter along major rivers, large lakes, and tidal areas throughout New Hampshire. Unfortunately, much of the land along the rivers is privately owned and not accessible to the public.

NEW JERSEY

Delaware Water Gap National Recreation Area

Bald eagles winter in the upper Delaware region, between East Stroudsburg and Port Jervis. 25 or more birds visible. Best viewing: from Delaware River bridges and river roads in New Jersey and Pennsylvania Jan. through Feb. Boat access possible. Water Gap managed by National Park Service, but associated areas along river mostly privately owned. Stay on public roads and lands. Contact: Delaware Water Gap National Recreation Area 570-426-2452.

Dividing Creek

Up to 20 bald eagles winter in the area of the marsh at Maple St., just W of town on Dividing Creek in S New Jersey Jan. through Feb.; subadult eagles and local fledglings may be in area June through Aug. Best viewing: from car, stop along road. From Millville, take County 555 to County 553 into Dividing Creek. Contact: New Jersey Endangered and Nongame Species Program 609-628-2103.

Edwin B. Forsythe National Wildlife Refuge, Brigantine Unit

A half dozen bald eagles winter in this area N of Atlantic City Jan. to Feb.; 2 to 3 eagles nest near but not on the refuge. Best viewing: from 8-mile auto tour (for a small per-car fee) around 2 impoundments adjacent to a salt marsh. Interpretive displays at visitor center. Take exit 41 off Garden State Pkwy., then Jim Leeds Rd. or Creek Rd. E to State Rt. 9. Entrance E of Rt. 9 in Oceanville. Contact: Forsythe National Wildlife Refuge 609-652-1665.

Manasquan Reservoir Bald Eagle Nest

An eagle nest is viewable from the Manasquan Reservoir Environmental Center. Eagles are present nearly year-round on the reservoir itself. Environmental Center is on Rt. 195, Georgia Tavern Rd., Howell, Ocean County. Contact: Manasquan Reservoir Environmental Center 732-751-9453.

Maurice River/Delaware Bay

Bald eagles winter at this site in Cumberland County Dec. through Feb., peaking at 20 to 40 in Jan. Access points from NJ 47 just S of NJ 55 include Mauricetown Bridge near Mauricetown, and roads from Port Elizabeth, Dorchester, and Leesburg, which end at river. Some viewing from Delaware Bay marshes, including Thompson's Beach (take old Rt. 47 to Glade Rd. to Thompson's Beach Rd.). Contact: New Jersey Endangered and Nongame Species Program 609-628-2103.

Stow Creek Bald Eagle Nest

A single pair of bald eagles has nested in Canton on the border of Salem and Cumberland counties Feb. through early Aug. Remain on roads; no access allowed in fields or private land. Viewing area available off New Bridge Rd., but eagles shift nest sites from year to year, and some are difficult to see. Access via NJ 49 and county roads from Salem. Contact: New Jersey Endangered and Nongame Species Program 609-628-2103.

NEW MEXICO

Bosque del Apache National Wildlife Refuge

About a dozen eagles follow the 30,000 or more snow geese that pile into this 57,200-acre refuge along the Rio Grande near Socorro. They loiter Nov. through mid-Feb., scavenging crippled and dead waterfowl in the extensive bottomlands and managed wetlands. Get a map at the visitor center, then take either of 2 tour loops (small fee). From I-24, take exit 139 E about .5 mile; take right on NM 1, and then 8 miles S to visitor center on right. Contact: Bosque del Apache National Wildlife Refuge 505-835-1828.

Cochiti Reservoir

About 9 bald eagles (and an occasional golden) winter around this reservoir on the Rio Grande, between Albuquerque and Santa Fe. Peak season Dec. through Feb. Best viewing: below the spillway. Dam top is open to foot traffic.

I-25, exit 259 (NM 22) NW for 9.8 miles; turn right on dirt road 1.8 miles; left onto Dam Crest Road, 1.3 miles to dam. Contact: U.S. Army Corps of Engineers 505-465-2300.

Conchas Reservoir

About 40 bald eagles winter Nov. through Feb. on this 25-mile-long 9,600-acre reservoir NW of Tucumcari in east-central New Mexico, operated by U.S. Army Corps of Engineers. Best viewing: from boat. The lake's many arms and limited road access make roadside and shore viewing difficult. On NM 104, head for settlement of Conchas until you reach the reservoir. Limited roads to SE and south-central areas of lake. Contact: Conchas Lake State Park 505-868-2270.

Elephant Butte Lake State Park

Dozens of bald eagles winter on this 36,500-acre, 43-mile-long lake S of Albuquerque. Best viewing: Nov. to Mar. by boat and from dirt roads. 7 miles N of Truth or Consequences on I-25. Contact: Elephant Butte Lake State Park 505-744-5421.

El Vado and Heron Reservoirs

Up to 20 bald eagles winter Nov. through Feb. on these twin lakes near the Colorado border, N of Santa Fe, which cover 5,900 acres. Best viewing: from boat; limited access from shore. 14 miles SW of Tierra Amarilla on NM 112 to El Vado. Drive 11 miles W of Tierra Amarilla on US 64 and NM 95 to Heron. State parks at each reservoir. Contact: Heron Lake State Park 505-588-7470.

Maxwell Lake National Wildlife Refuge

The refuge and its three lakes in NE New Mexico are on the migration corridor on the front range of the Rocky Mountains. The middle lake, Lake 13, has offered views of up to 30 bald eagles Nov. through Mar. Exit I-25 at mile marker 426 and go W 2 blocks into Maxwell. Go 0.75 mile N on NM 445, then W on NM 505 2.5 miles to entrance. Headquarters 1.25 miles N. Contact: U.S. Fish and Wildlife Service 505-375-2331.

McAllister Lake/Las Vegas National Wildlife Refuge

These adjoining areas NE of Albuquerque provide habitat for migrating waterfowl and about 25 wintering bald eagles Nov. through Mar. McAllister Lake open year-round; the refuge is less accessible. Viewing from car or on foot. From I-25 at S edge of Las Vegas, turn E on NM 104 1.2 miles. Turn S (right) on NM 281 4 miles to refuge office, another 0.5 mile to Crane Lake Overlook, and 3 more miles to McAllister Lake. Contact: (McAllister Lake), New Mexico Dept. of Game and Fish 505-445-2311; Las Vegas National Wildlife Refuge 505-425-3581.

Navajo Reservoir

Up to 50 bald eagles winter Nov. through Feb. on this 15,000-acre lake in NW New Mexico, E of Farmington. Best viewing: Dec. through Feb. by boat along hundreds of miles of shoreline. 25 miles E of Bloomfield on US 64 and NM 511. Contact: Navajo Lake State Park 505-632-2278, Bureau of Reclamation 505-632-3115.

Rio Grande Nature Center State Park

During fall and winter, migrating eagles, sandhill cranes, and waterfowl lay over in the cottonwood forest along the Rio Grande in and near Albuquerque. At least one pair has nested in summer. 2 miles of nature trails along river, from which to view eagles. From I-40 take exit 157A onto Rio Grande Blvd. N for three blocks, turn left onto Candelaria Rd.; from I-25 take exit 227 (frontage road) and turn right onto Candelaria Rd. State park is at the W end of Candelaria. Contact: Rio Grande Nature Center 505-344-7240.

Ute Reservoir

With 8,200 acres, many arms and inlets, and little road access, Ute Reservoir provides safe winter haven for about 45 bald eagles from Nov. through Feb. Best viewing: from boat in the upper portions of the lake where large snags provide roosts, NE of Tucumcari (near Texas border), 3 miles W of Logan via NM 540. Contact: Ute Lake State Park 505-487-2284, New Mexico Game and Fish 505-445-2311.

NEW YORK

Iroquois National Wildlife Refuge

One of two recent nesting pairs on this 10,800-acre refuge is visible from refuge headquarters. Best viewing: Apr. through June. N of Batavia off NY 63 (in town of Alabama). Contact: Iroquois National Wildlife Refuge 585-948-5445.

Lower Hudson River

Wintering eagles and about a dozen nesting pairs use the lower Hudson.

Much of the stretch from Kingston to Croton is kept open by discharges from power plants, and railroad tracks provide an ample supply of dead animals for scavenging birds. Best viewing: Norrie Point State Park, Constitution Island from North Dock, US 6-202 overlook above Iona Island, Riverfront Park in Peekskill, Charles Point and China Pier in Peekskill, Verplank waterfront, and George's Island Park parking area in Verplank. Metro-North and Amtrack commuters on the river side of any train between Albany and Croton-on-Hudson stand a good chance of spotting eagles.

Montezuma National Wildlife Refuge

In summer, up to 60 bald eagles frequent this 10,000-acre refuge in central New York; 3 pairs are known to nest. Good viewing from observation tower at Tschache Pool, a shallow waterfowl impoundment. Some eagles stay the winter. Maps and brochures available at the visitor center, staffed part-time. W of Syracuse off I-90. Contact: Montezuma National Wildlife Refuge 315-568-5987.

St. Lawrence River

Up to 50 bald eagles winter early Dec. through mid-Mar. on the open water of the St. Lawrence River along the New

York–Canada border. Best viewing: Jan. through mid-Feb. from auto along NY 12 on U.S. side of river, from Rt. 401 on Canada side. Look for open water and flocks of gulls and waterfowl, especially Chippewa Bay, Wellesley Island, Ivy Lea, and Brockville Narrows. Drive along the U.S. shore of the river from the Thousand Islands Bridge E to Massena and Robert Moses State Park. Contact: New York State Dept. of Environmental Conservation, Wildlife Office, Waterton 315-265-3090.

Sullivan County

A wintering area for up to 100 eagles in southern New York S of the Catskill Mountains. Best viewing: Jan. through mid-Feb. from Rio Reservoir or Monguap Falls Reservoir, where there's a public viewing blind, and the Upper Delaware River. View from public roads around both reservoirs and from NY 97 along Delaware River. The Eagle Institute in Barryville staff the platform with volunteers in the blind and with scopes. Contact: Eagle Institute 845-557-6162 or 570-685-5960.

NORTH CAROLINA

Jordan Lake

Bald eagles nest and overwinter on Jordan Lake, a reservoir on the Haw River. Numbers range from fewer than a dozen in winter to about 20 in summer. Principal access from US 64 causeway over lake W of Raleigh and E of Pittsboro. Parking lot turnoff 6.7 miles N of US 64. Marked trail 0.7 mile to observation deck. Contact: U. S. Army Corps of Engineers 919-542-4501, Jordan Lake State Recreation Area 919-362-0586.

NORTH DAKOTA

Garrison Dam National Fish Hatchery Outflow Channel

View wintering bald eagles near the hatchery and dam N of Bismarck. Permanent blind for viewing and photography. From Riverdale, take ND 200 W over Garrison Dam spillway (about 1 mile) and follow signs toward downstream campgrounds. Park along campground road at S end of hatchery. Walk W cross-country (no marked trail) about 200 yards. Contact: Garrison Dam National Fish Hatchery 701-654-7451.

Riverdale Wildlife Management Area

2,197 acres of forest and grassland near the Missouri River. More than 15 wintering bald eagles visible from trail or along river from mid-Dec. through Feb. Portable blinds welcome. Foot traffic only; vehicle traffic prohibited. From Riverdale, go W on ND 200 to gravel road just before Garrison Dam spillway (about 0.5 mile); turn S. Road gradually turns W; take second road that turns S for 0.5 mile; turn E or W to management area. From parking lot, follow service road trail S 0.5 mile. Trail turns W toward river for another 0.75 mile. Contact: North Dakota Game and Fish Dept. 701-654-7475.

OHIO

Ottawa National Wildlife Refuge Complex

More than two dozen eagles are visible on the 9,000-acre area during late summer as fledgling eagles congregate. Best viewing: Aug. through Sept. from walking trails along Crane Creek. In spring, nest visible from visitor center. Off OH 2, 15 miles E of Toledo. Contact: Ottawa National Wildlife Refuge Visitor Center 419-898-0014.

Pickerel Creek State Wildlife Area

More than a dozen adult and fledgling eagles gather Aug. through Sept. on these 3,300 acres SE of Toledo. Best viewing: from roads around area and just inside entrance. 2 active nests in spring. Many eagles remain till well into winter. Off US 6 about 8 miles E of Fremont. Contact: Pickerel Creek State Wildlife Area 419-547-6007, Crane Creek Wildlife Research Station 419-898-0960.

OKLAHOMA

More than 1,000 eagles winter on Oklahoma's lakes and rivers. Lakes with greatest numbers include Kaw, Texoma, Tenkiller, Ft. Gibson, Grand, Canton, Great Salt Plains, Eufaula, and Spavinaw. Contact: Oklahoma Wildlife Diversity Program 405-521-2739. (For information, check www.wildlifedepartment.com/eagleviewing.htm, which contains a tour schedule updated each winter.)

Broken Bow Reservoir

Eagles nest and winter on 14,000-acre Broken Bow Reservoir in SE Oklahoma. One place to see them is the 5,400-acre Broken Bow Wildlife Management Area, at the N (upstream) end of the lake. Contact: Broken Bow Reservoir Management Area 580-241-7875. At the other end, near the dam, is Beavers Bend Resort Park. Sightings of eagles fishing below dam during winter. Peak viewing: Dec. to Jan. 7 miles N of Broken Bow on Hwy. 259, then 4 miles E on Hwy. 259A. Contact: Beavers Bend Nature Center 580-494-6556.

Tishomingo National Wildlife Refuge

About a dozen eagles winter on the 16,500-acre refuge in S Oklahoma, picking off migrating waterfowl from the Central Flyway. From downtown Tishomingo, follow OK 78 to the E edge of town. Turn S on Refuge Rd. at the high school (watch for sign). Follow Refuge Rd. 3 miles to headquarters. Contact: Tishomingo National Wildlife Refuge 580-371-2402.

Washita National Wildlife Refuge

Bald eagles follow migrating waterfowl to the 8,200-acre Washita National Wildlife Refuge each fall. A good place to look for eagles, as well as sandhill cranes and waterfowl: the deck at Owl Cove, where the lazy Washita River enters the Foss Reservoir. Also, the observation deck behind the office. Headquarters and office located 5 miles W of Butler on OK 33, then 1 mile N and 0.5 mile W. Contact: Washita National Wildlife Refuge 580-664-2205.

OREGON

Bear Valley National Wildlife Refuge

This 4,178-acre valley, part of the larger Klamath Basin National Wildlife Refuges Complex (see California) is a night roosting area for wintering bald eagles. Watch the "fly-out" at dawn when eagles head to Lower Klamath to feed. Approximately 300 eagles Dec. through Feb. Take US 97 S from Worden. Turn W onto road to Keno (after Worden Café). Cross railroad tracks and take unmarked gravel road to little valley leading into Bear Valley. You can watch the fly-out from your car. Contact: Klamath Basin National Wildlife Refuges Complex 530-667-2231.

Crane Prairie Reservoir

Several pairs of bald eagles nest in this 10,600-acre site in the Cascade Mountains in Deschutes National Forest. Pairs remain year-round. Best viewing: late Apr. through Sept. from boat, also from docks or lakeshore. Hiking trail leads to reservoir. S 15 miles from Bend on US 97. Turn right at Sunriver turnoff (Forest Rd. 40) for 21 miles to Forest Rd. 46. Turn S and watch for campgrounds. Trail to reservoir begins 0.5 mile S of Quinn River Campground on Forest Rd. 46. Contact: Deschutes National Forest 541-383-5300.

Klamath Basin Winter Wings Festival

Four-day eagle-watching event every President's Day weekend that opens in downtown Klamath Falls with arts, food, music, expert-led tours, workshops, and other attractions. Contact: www.winterwingsfest.org.

Oak Springs Fish Hatchery

Up to a half dozen bald eagles fish and roost in the tall trees in this steep canyon along the Deschutes River S of The Dalles. (A pair of goldens has taken residence as well.) Numbers peak in Jan. Best viewing: park car just before railroad tracks, or view from fish hatchery. From Maupin drive 6 miles

N on US 197. Turn E 3 miles at fish hatchery sign. Contact: Oak Springs Fish Hatchery 541-395-2546.

Sauvie Island Wildlife Area

Up to 80 wintering bald eagles visit this 12,000-acre area Dec. through Mar. to feed on waterfowl and fish. A half dozen pairs nest on the refuge Jan. through late June. Best viewing: from Reeder Rd., which parallels refuge. To wildlife area, go W 10 miles from Portland on US 30. Cross Sauvie Island Bridge and travel N 2 miles. Headquarters on right just past the NW Reeder Rd. junction. Entry restricted Oct. to Apr. 15 to prevent disturbance to waterfowl. Contact: Sauvie Island Wildlife Area 503-621-3488.

Twilight Creek Eagle Sanctuary

The sanctuary's observation platform provides a stunning view of the lower Columbia River estuary. Nesting and wintering eagles forage over thousands of acres of mudflats, tidal marshes, open water, and islands. To platform, take old Hwy. 30 to Burnside (between Svensen and the John Day River). Respect private property. Contact: North Coast Land Conservancy 503-717-2298.

Upper Crooked Bald Eagle Viewing Tour

As many as 50 wintering bald eagles congregate in the Upper Crooked River valley NE of Bend Dec. through Apr. Numbers peak in Mar. Best viewing: from the Paulina Hwy., look for eagles in trees along river or soaring overhead. Go E 1 mile from Prineville on US 26. Turn S on the Paulina Hwy. 25 miles past Post following the Crooked River.

PENNSYLVANIA

Middle Creek Wildlife Management Area

Adult and immature bald eagles are visible year-around on this 6,254-acre area N of Lancaster. In midsummer, 2 to 3 eagles may be viewed from visitor center or from auto tour pullouts around Middle Creek Lake. Look for birds on snags in lake. From PA turnpike, take exit 21 onto PA 272 N 3 miles to traffic light. Left on PA 897 N about 14 miles to Kleinfeltersville. After stop sign, left onto Hopeland Rd. for 2 miles to visitor center. Contact: Middle Creek Visitor Center 717-733-1512.

Pymatuning Reservoir

Nearly a dozen pairs of bald eagles begin nesting on the state's largest lake (17,100 acres) in Feb., and most remain year-round. Possibility of seeing a couple dozen adult and immature eagles. Peak viewing of nests in Apr. Viewing platforms, volunteers, and spotting scopes at Pymatuning Wildlife Learning Center. Educational programs and tours available. Take I-79 from Erie to Meadville exit. Go to Conneaut Lake and on to Linesville. At light, turn left and go 0.5 mile past hatchery to entrance. Contact: Pymatuning Wildlife Learning Center 814-683-5545.

RHODE ISLAND

Bald eagles are seen year-round in Rhode Island, especially on Scituate Reservoir, where eagles nest and overwinter. Birds have nested on an island visible from Rt. 116 on E side of reservoir, about 1 mile S of North Scituate (at junction of Rts. 116 and 6). Contact: Rhode Island Audubon Society 401-949-5454.

SOUTH CAROLINA

ACE Basin

Nearly 40 pairs of bald eagles nest Feb. through Apr. at the confluence of the Ashepoo, Combahee, and Edisto rivers on the Atlantic coast, an area known as the ACE Basin. A few of the nests are on the 11,800-acre Ernest F. Hollings ACE Basin National Wildlife Refuge. Other major public holdings are the 11,000-acre Bear Island Wildlife Management Area and 8,500-acre Donnelly Wildlife Management Area. The

Nature Conservancy also has several conservation easement agreements with private land owners. Contact: ACE Basin National Wildlife Refuge 843-889-3084, Bear Island and Donnelly 843-844-8957.

Santee Cooper Lakes

Up to 40 pairs of bald eagles nest around the Cooper River and Lakes Marion and Moultrie, SE of Columbia. Best viewing: Feb. and Mar. from shoreline, Santee Dam, and hiking trails in designated areas. Trail access to lakes from 2,828-acre Santee Cooper Wildlife Management Area and 15,000-acre Santee National Wildlife Refuge. Contact: Santee National Wildlife Refuge 803-478-2217, state wildlife area 803-655-5809, Santee Cooper Property Management 843-761-4068.

SOUTH DAKOTA

Karl E. Mundt National Wildlife Refuge/Fort Randall Dam

From Oct. through Feb., bald eagles winter at the refuge and dam along the Missouri River in SE South Dakota. The refuge, one of the most important eagle winter roosts in the region, is closed to the public, but an interpretive sign is located downriver from powerhouse below dam, where 50 to 200 (depending on severity of winter) eagles congregate in a 3-mile stretch to feed on fish and waterfowl. Numbers peak Jan. through Feb. From Pickstown, travel W on US 46, cross Fort Randall Dam, and go to powerhouse below dam. Just before security gate, turn right on blacktop road heading downriver (S) about 0.25 mile. Road dead-ends at interpretive sign. Contact: Karl E. Mundt National Wildlife Refuge 605-487-7603, U.S. Army Corps of Engineers 605-487-7845.

Oahe Dam

About two dozen bald eagles frequent two areas below Oahe Dam on the Missouri River early Nov. through mid-Mar. Numbers and peak times depend on weather and influx of wintering geese. By car, go through Downstream North (800 acres) campgrounds to view eagles along river. Downstream South (60 acres) is closed to all but foot traffic; park at closed gate and walk down road to water to see eagles feeding or perched in trees across river. Eagle Awareness Day yearly in early Jan.; educational and guided viewing opportunities. Oahe Dam is 6 miles N of Pierre on SD 1804 or SD 1806. Contact: U.S. Army Corps of Engineers 605-224-5862.

TENNESSEE

Dale Hollow Lake

A 27,000-acre lake with winter viewing of up to 50 eagles Oct. through Mar. Best viewing: from 7.3-mile trail between Willow Grove and Lillydale Recreation areas on S side of lake. U.S. Army Corps of Engineers offers viewing tours in Jan. On I-40 E from Nashville, take exit 280. Travel N on TN 56 through Gainesboro. Turn N on TN 53 through Celina; follow signs to resource manager's office. Contact: U.S. Army Corps of Engineers 931-243-3136.

Land Between the Lakes

More than 20 nesting pairs and 100 wintering eagles frequent the 300 miles of undeveloped shoreline of the peninsula straddling the Tennessee and Cumberland river valleys in W Tennessee. Viewing by boat or car. Peak concentration Dec. through Jan. Annual Eagle Weekends in Feb. From I-24, go W on US 79, 37 miles through Clarksville, across Cumberland River Bridge, and through Dover to S entrance. Turn right (N) on TN 100 (The Trace) about 3 miles to S welcome station. Golden Pond Visitor Center and Planetarium about 20 miles farther N. Contact: Land Between the Lakes National Recreation Area 270-924-2000.

Reelfoot Lake

Up to 300 bald eagles winter along the shore of 16,000-acre Reelfoot Lake, near the Missouri border. Peak numbers

Dec. through Feb. Reelfoot Lake State Park has winter eagle-viewing tours by bus (best viewing Feb.), pontoon boat tours (spring through fall), and driving and hiking areas. From Tiptonville, drive 2.6 miles E on TN 21/22 to visitor center on left. Contact: Reelfoot Lake State Park Visitor Center 731-253-9652, Reelfoot National Wildlife Refuge 731-538-2481.

TEXAS

Fairfield Lake

About a dozen bald eagles winter in this 1,400-acre park SE of Dallas. Best viewing: by boat Nov. through Feb. Viewing from shore also possible with binoculars or spotting scope. From I-45 take US 84 E to Fairfield. Drive 6 miles NE on FM 488 and FM 2570 to park road 64. Contact: Fairfield Lake State Park 903-389-4514.

Lake Buchanan

Bald eagles and other species of migrating birds winter at 23,500-acre Lake Buchanan NW of Austin. Best viewing: by boat. Several public boat ramps on lake. Vanishing Texas River Cruise offers tours on Canyon of the Eagles for fee. Reservations recommended. To dock for cruises, go 3 miles W of Burnet on TX 29 and N on FM 2341, 13.5 miles to entrance. Contact: Canyon of the Eagles Tours 512-756-6986.

Lake Fork Reservoir

This 27,700-acre reservoir attracts about 80 bald eagles from Nov. to Mar. Viewing from shore or boat. Take US 80 E from Dallas to Mineola, TX 37 N to Quitman, TX 154 W to dam. Contact: Sabine River Authority 903-878-2262.

Lake o' the Pines

More than 30 bald eagles winter at this 18,700-acre lake in the state's NE corner near Louisiana. Best viewing: from dam overlook, also from boat or shore. From TX 49 NW from Jefferson take US 59 W about 3 miles. Go W on FM 729 to FM 726. Turn S on 726 to dam and S shore parks, or stay on 729 W to N shore parks. Contact: Lake o' the Pines Chamber of Commerce 903-755-2597 or 877-347-4567.

UTAH

Farmington Bay Waterfowl Management Area

200 to 400 bald eagles winter Nov. through Mar. at this 18,000-acre site in N Utah. Auto and walking routes; tours and educational talks. Take W Bountiful exit off I-15 and follow signs to area. Contact: Farmington Bay Waterfowl Management Area 801-451-7386.

Ogden Bay Waterfowl Management Area

Up to 100 bald eagles visit this 20,000-acre site in N Utah Nov. through Mar. Walking tours. Take exit 341 (Roy) off I-15 and get on UT 97 W until it ends. Go N on UT 108 for 0.1 mile and W on UT 98 to Hooper. Continue W on 5500 S, then N on 7500 W. Contact: Ogden Bay Waterfowl Management Area 801-985-1398.

Ouray National Wildlife Refuge

Up to 100 bald eagles come mid-Nov. through early Jan., then return late Feb. through Mar., settling along the 12-mile stretch of the Green River in this 12,000-acre refuge in NE Utah. They remain all winter if it is mild and the water does not freeze over. Best viewing: from 9.5-mile auto tour route. Go 14 miles W from Vernal on US 40 and turn S on UT 88 for 16 miles to headquarters. Contact: Ouray National Wildlife Refuge 435-545-2522.

Pariette Wetlands

About a dozen eagles winter at this 9,033-acre marsh and desert upland complex in NW Utah. (Numbers have dropped because of prolonged drought.) Best viewing: late Oct. through Nov. and late Feb. through early Mar., from gravel and dirt roads throughout the area. Stay off gated roads. Take US 40 to Fort Duchesne and turn S about 5 miles (just past Duchesne River). At the Myton Y turn S off of road to Myton onto dirt road for 16 miles across Leland Bench to Pariette. Follow signs to overlook. Inquire first about road conditions. Contact: Bureau of Land Management 435-781-4400.

Rush Lake

From Nov. through Mar., bald eagles visit this wetland (up to 6 miles long and 2 wide when water is high). Eagles perch in dead trees along road and roost on E side of lake along UT 36. Excellent viewing from highway, which is elevated. Do not stop on road; use pullouts. Bald eagle activities in winter. From Tooele take UT 36 S to Stockton. Continue on UT 36. Contact: Bureau of Land Management 801-977-4300.

Salt Creek Waterfowl Management Area

Up to 50 bald eagles visit this 7,050-acre site in N Utah Nov. through Mar. Auto and walking routes. Good viewing of entire area from Compton's Knoll with spotting scope or binoculars. From Corrine go W 8 miles on UT 83. Turn N on gravel surface 3.5 miles to entrance. Continue 1.2 miles to Compton's Knoll. Contact: Salt Creek Waterfowl Management Area 801-854-3610.

Willard Bay–Harold Crane Waterfowl Management Area

Up to 50 bald eagles winter at this 12,500-acre site in N Utah Nov. through Mar. Good viewing from walking routes. From I-15 take exit 354 (Willard Bay, Pleasant View). Turn W on 4000 N and drive to S marina of Willard Bay; walk-in access only. For vehicle access, drive to end of 4000 N to gravel road. Additional access: from I-15 take exit 347 to UT 39 W. Turn N on 6700 W to walk-in access. Contact: Willard Bay–Harold Crane Waterfowl Management Area 801-510-1406.

VERMONT

Dead Creek Wildlife Management Area

In this 2,900-acre wildlife management area near Lake Champlain, Dead Creek has been impounded to form cattail-dominated wetlands for waterfowl. Wintering bald eagles feed on fish that die from oxygen depletion in these shallow frozen ponds. Best viewing: Mar. as ice melts. From Addison, go W on Rt. 17, 1.6 miles to parking lot on left. You can continue W on Rt. 17, 0.6 mile over Dead Creek to Brilyea Access Rd. on left. Drive to the end of the access road as you look for eagles. Contact: Dead Creek Management Area 802-759-2398.

Harriman Station

Several eagles spend Dec. through Apr. below a dam on the Deerfield River W of Brattleboro. On I-91, take exit 3. Go W 20 miles until road crosses Deerfield River in Readsboro. Travel S on River Rd 1 mile. Contact: Vermont Dept. of Fish and Wildlife 802-241-3700.

Lake Champlain Ferry Landings

Ferry traffic keeps landing ice free, attracting wintering bald eagles. Two good bets for eagle watchers are the Charlotte Ferry Landing (McNeil Cove) and the Grand Isle Ferry Landing.

North Monroe Bridge

About 11 bald eagles summer on the island S of this bridge July through Aug. The bridge spans the Connecticut River at the N end of McIndoes Reservoir, S of St. Johnsbury. Take exit 18 off I-91. Go S on US 5, 0.25 mile. North Monroe Bridge on left. Pullout before bridge; park and walk across bridge to view. Viewing also good from adjacent roads, NH 135, and roads between E. Barnet and Lower Waterford.

Vernon, Bellows Falls, and Wilder Dams

These hydroelectric dams, all within 75 miles of each other, keep water on the Connecticut River open all winter. One or two eagles below each dam any time Dec. through Apr. Vernon Dam (S of Brattleboro): take I-91 to US 5 and go N; turn S on VT 142, 7 miles to dam. Bellows Falls Dam: in downtown Bellows Falls off US 5. Wilder Dam (near White River Junction): take exit 12 off I-91. Follow US 5 N 1.9 miles. Turn right on Depot St., left on Norwich St., and right on Passumpsic Ave.

VIRGINIA

Caledon Natural Area

Several dozen bald eagles roost mid-June through early Sept. along the shoreline of these 2,579 acres on the Potomac River E of Fredericksburg. Ranger-led tours (for a fee) mid-June through Labor Day. Arrange group tours in advance. From US 301 in King George County, take VA 206 W 4 miles to VA 218 W. About 1 mile to park. Contact: Caledon Natural Area 540-663-3861.

James River National Wildlife Refuge

Several eagle pairs nest in this 4,200-acre refuge along the James River, created in 1991 to protect eagle nesting and roosting habitat. Up to 70 eagles are visible late some summers. The Nature Conservancy purchased 3,538 acres of land in May 1988. The U.S. Fish and Wildlife Service purchased the land from the Nature Conservancy in Mar. 1991 under the authority of the Endangered Species Act. Additional land was added to the refuge in 1992. From Richmond, take I-295 S to Rt. 10. Take Rt. 10 SE toward Hopewell. After passing through Hopewell, proceed another 8 miles to Rt. 639. Take a left and look for the refuge entrance sign. Contact: James River National Wildlife Refuge 804-829-9020 or 804-333-1470.

Mason Neck National Wildlife Refuge/Mason Neck State Park

A half dozen nesting pairs visit the 8,000-acre peninsula on the Potomac River S of Alexandria. More than 200 birds may spend winter and spring on the 60 miles of river from Mount Vernon to Aquia Creek. Best viewing: in refuge from Great Marsh Trail, in park from Bay View and Kane's Creek trails. At junction with US 1, go E on VA 242 (Gunston Rd.) to wildlife refuge. Follow High Point Rd., to right, to state park. Contact: Mason Neck National Wildlife Refuge 703-490-4979, park 703-339-2385.

WASHINGTON

Methow Wildlife Area

Hundreds of bald eagles nest in the Methow River watershed, including these 14,500 acres of shrub-steppe and forest habitats W of Colville Indian Reservation. Also 2 active nests in the valley. Best winter viewing between Winthrop and Twisp. Take WA 153 to WA 20. Turn NW to Twisp and on to Winthrop. Contact: Methow Wildlife Area 509-996-2559.

North Fork Nooksack River

Bald eagles concentrate along the 10 miles of the Nooksack River (E of Bellingham) from Kendall to Deming Oct. to Mar. Peaks of more than 100 Dec. to early Jan. Best viewing: from Nooksack Salmon Hatchery and Welcome Bridge on Mosquito Lake Rd. From Kendall go 1 mile S on North Fork Rd. to hatchery; bridge 5 miles farther S. *Do not park in front of Welcome Fire Station.* Contact: North Fork Nooksack River Hatchery 360-676-2138.

San Juan Island: Cattle Point

The San Juan Islands have one of the highest densities of nesting bald eagles in the lower forty-eight (some 120 nesting pairs). Many remain year-round. Good viewing from Cattle

Point on San Juan Island. Look for birds roosting in tall trees or soaring near channel between San Juan and Lopez islands. From Friday Harbor, take San Juan Valley Rd. SW, S on Douglas Rd., W on Little Rd. Take Cattle Point Rd. S to Cattle Point. Nest on Cattle Point (with parking area nearby). Also look for nest near driveway of American Camp Visitor Center. Contact: San Juan Island National Historical Park 360-378-2902.

Skagit River Bald Eagle Natural Area

Bald eagle viewing Nov. through mid-Mar. on 8 miles of the Skagit River between Rockport and Marblemount. Largest concentration (over 450 in mid-Jan.) corresponds with chum salmon spawn. Best viewing: from Washington Eddy lookout 1 mile E of Rockport on WA 20, and a highway pullout 1.3 miles farther. Also from Skagit View Trail at Rockport State Park. Upper Skagit Bald Eagle Festival in January. Contact: Skagit River Interpretive Center 360-853-7283, www.skagiteagle.org.

WEST VIRGINIA

Potomac Eagle Train

The Potomac Eagle Scenic Railroad offers a 3-hour narrated train ride along the South Branch of the Potomac River. Train passes through narrow valley known as "the Trough." Bald eagles present year-round. Nests clearly visible May through June from train's open-air gondola. Rides year-round from Wappocomo Station, 1 mile N of Romney. Contact: Potomac Eagle Scenic Railroad 304-424-0736 or www.potomaceagle.info.

The National Conservation Training Center of the U.S. Fish and Wildlife Service near Shepherdstown is not open to the public, but it does maintain a live eagle cam during nesting season: www.fws.gov/nctc/cam.

WISCONSIN

Nelson Dewey State Park

More than 600 bald eagles may winter along the 100-mile stretch of the Mississippi River from La Crosse, WI, to Dubuque, IA. Nelson Dewey State Park and Cassville are on a 2-mile stretch where a Wisconsin Power and Light plant keeps water open all winter. Eagles present mid-Dec. through mid-Mar.; peak late Jan. through early Feb. In Cassville, view from platforms above river in park and from boat landing at S end of Riverside Park near old Dairyland Power Plant. Cassville's Bald Eagle Days last weekend in Jan. To park, take WI 133 N from Cassville. At edge of town turn left on County VV; entrance 1 mile on right. Contact: park 608-725-5374, Cassville Tourism 608-725-5855, or www.cassville.org/eagledays.

Petenwell Dam

Wintering bald eagles can be seen on open water below this dam on the Wisconsin River E of Tomah on WI 21. Three observation areas. Stop at parking areas E and W of bridge over Wisconsin River. Eagles visible upstream. Drive W from bridge; take 19th St. W about 0.2 mile, and 18th Ave. N for 0.75 mile. Look just below dam on W side of river for eagles.

Sauk Prairie Eagle Viewing Site

As many as 200 bald eagles winter mid-Dec. through mid-Feb. along the lower Wisconsin River 25 miles NW of Madison where a dam keeps water open. Observation platform with spotting scope; if not viewing from platform, please remain in car. Some weekends in peak season, volunteers provide interpretive information at platform. Near Sauk City, take US 12 N across Wisconsin River. Turn right immediately on Water St. for 1.4 miles to public parking lot in Prairie du Sac. Ferry Bluff Eagle Council sponsors Eagle Days in mid-Jan. Contact: Sauk Prairie Area Chamber of Commerce 608-643-4168, 800-683-2453, or www.saukprairie.com.

Upper Mississippi River Fish and Wildlife Refuge

Much of the bald eagle habitat along the Mississippi in Wisconsin, Minnesota, and Iowa lies within this refuge, which stretches along 261 miles of the river. More than 150 pairs nest in the refuge, and hundreds loiter in trees during the winter. The refuge is also a magnet for nesting white pelicans and migrating waterfowl, including tundra swans and canvasbacks. Contact: Upper Mississippi River Fish and Wildlife Refuge 888-291-5719.

WYOMING

Bighorn River

From Dec. through early Mar., about 25 to 50 bald eagles winter along a stretch of the Bighorn River from Greybull to Thermopolis, NW of Casper. Follow WY 433 along the river. US 20 connects Greybull and Thermopolis.

Buffalo Bill State Park

This 11,000-acre state park surrounds Buffalo Bill Reservoir, hangout of migrating eagles Mar. through Apr. and Oct. through Nov. Some also winter Nov. to Mar. Good viewing of perching birds from either end of reservoir on North and South forks of Shoshone River. Drive the North Fork Hwy. (US 14/16/20) of WY 1501 along the South Fork. Good viewing from gravel roads off these roads. Contact: Buffalo Bill State Park 307-587-9227.

Jackson Canyon

See a concentration of wintering bald eagles along the North Platte River from the Jackson Canyon pullout, off I-25 SW of Casper. A roost of about 50 eagles from mid-Nov. through mid-Mar. View from parking lot to avoid disturbing birds. Actual roost on private land.

Snake River

About 30 nesting pairs in summer and 50 to 100 birds in winter frequent a stretch of the Snake River just N and S of Jackson, from Jackson Lake to the Idaho border. In summer, float downriver through Grand Teton National Park to see eagles. Drive along US 191 N and S of Jackson, or on road along river in Grand Teton National Park. Pullouts along the way. Contact: Grand Teton National Park Headquarters 307-739-3300.

ABOUT THE PHOTOGRAPHER/AUTHOR

Frank Oberle, the premier photographer for this book, may be the most prolific bald eagle photographer in the country. *Audubon, Sports Illustrated, National Geographic, Nature Conservancy,* and *National Wildlife* are just a few of the publications in which his eagle images have appeared. Shooting photos like Oberle's takes as much patience as it does skill. Oberle's images capture perfectly the grace, artistry, and beauty of bald eagles.

Greg Breining has traveled the world to write stories on subjects as diverse as bison, fossils, and canoes for *The New York Times, Sports Illustrated, Nature Conservancy, Audubon, Wildlife Conservation, Islands,* and other magazines. His other books include *Wild Shore* and *Super Volcano.*